DREAMS

★ ★ ★ FROM OUR ★ ★ ★

FATHERS

DREAMS
★ ★ ★ FROM OUR ★ ★ ★
FATHERS

DANA J. BAHAN

GRATUITY

Gratuity
Direct Number: 2134389957
(888) 290-0987
9350 Wilshire Blvd, Suite 203,
Beverly Hills, CA 90212

Published by Gratuity: 09/05/2024

ISBN: 978-1-965386-04-0(sc)
ISBN: 978-1-965386-05-7(e)

CONTENTS

CHAPTER 7

CHAPTER 8

CHAPTER 9

CHAPTER 10

ABOUT THE BOOK

*I*n the Author Forward of my book I try to make it abundantly clear that as a Christian to make a protest of government intrusion in our lives whether it be higher taxes or burdensome policies, it must be done peacefully. As a Christian it is my responsibility to be subject to governing authorities; but it is also a my right as part of the governed to question decisions made by government officials that endanger Constitutional and inalienable God given rights.

So, in the book I bring forth evidence from former Presidents and founding fathers who believed and trusted in the God of the Bible, who at times referred to him as "Nature's God." I make the assertion that our country was blessed and prospered because of these great men, but not just because of man's wisdom and virtue alone. I make the assertion that the Constitution and Declaration of Independence were and are still great documents, and should not be re-written, done away with or ignored by elected government officials, and should be held accountable to the oath they took to uphold it to the American people they represent.

I try to encourage all people who love this country as founded, to pray for our leaders and to vote responsibly and not along party lines solely, because excessive allegiance to one party can lead towards corruption. I encourage Christians to take active roles in politics, because if they are faithful I believe God will use them to bless society.

I believe God will bless our nation when we vote for responsible people of high moral character whether they be Christian or not, religious or non-religious. Three things that must be common for all public officials. They must be free from the "love of money," they must follow the Constitution, and they must be active to preserve and protect our freedoms.

I warn about the dangers of socialism and Marxism ideology, and how it has permeated our culture, education, and our government. I speak of President Obama's actions back in 2012, and reminding citizens of words that he spoke, and trying to interpret their meaning. He spoke the words of wanting to "Fundamentally Transform America." I spoke of his associations with a terrorist, and also with a church of Black Theology clergyman who often spoke about his hate for America. I spoke of his actions and words spoke in questioning and discrediting law enforcement during incidents with a black professor, and during riots in cities. I reminded readers of how an obliging media ignored informing the American public of his associations before his election, and continued to do so during his terms in office. I also gave opinion that he created a kind of social unrest and racial disharmony in riots and protests.

I encourage our nations continued support for the nation of Israel, a nation much like ours. Israel being the only country in the middle-east that has free elections, and has proven to be a strong ally to the United States. From scripture in the book of Jeremiah, "any nation that blesses Israel will be blessed, but any nation that curses Israel will be cursed."

ABRAHAM LINCOLN'S PRAYER

*I*n 1863, during the American Civil War, Abraham Lincoln called the nation to prayer based upon God's promise in II Chronicles 7:14. He said, "We have been the recipients of the choicest bounties of Heaven. We have been preserved, these many years, in peace and prosperity. We have grown in numbers, wealth and power, as no other nation has ever grown. But we have forgotten God. We have forgotten the gracious hand which preserved us in peace, and multiplied and enriched and strengthened us; and we have vainly imagined, in the deceitfulness of our hearts, that all these blessings were produced by some superior wisdom and virtue of our own. Intoxicated with unbroken success, we have become too self-sufficient to feel the necessity of redeeming and preserving grace, too proud to pray to the God that made us! It behooves us then, to humble ourselves before the offended Power, to confess our national sins, and to pray for clemency and forgiveness."

Interestingly, this great Bible verse was respected and quoted by three presidents; George Washington, Abraham Lincoln, and Ronald Reagan. Just what was this great Bible verse? "Then if my people who are called by my name will humble themselves and pray and seek my face and turn from their wicked ways, I will hear from heaven and will forgive their sins and heal their land." II Chronicles 7:14

WAKE UP CHURCH

"Where two or more are gathered together in my name, " is considered to be a church, if the name they are honoring is Jesus Christ, In II Chronicles 7:14, God is clear when he speaks in this verse that it is imperative that "His people who are called by His name," will humble themselves and turn away from sin and wickedness, that God will hear from heaven and forgive their sins and heal their land."

I have a strong conviction that churches must stand apart and stand against ungodliness in all its form in our culture. This does not mean disengaged. To stand apart to me means not being complicit or approving, or to be silent about ungodliness in a "woke movement" advocating alternative lifestyles, redefining genders, or justifying abortions even up to the time of birth. As well, standing against an intrusive government that attempt to steal away our God given freedoms. People of faith must be "salt and light" to have a heart change to be like Christ. We need the boldness to speak truth in love, to be kind and patient, and a bit vulnerable in recognizing we are human and we make mistakes like everybody else, but hopefully not as blatant as the godless. Without God's Son, Jesus Christ and His Spirit, and His power, we are just a loud noise or an annoyance to those we try to guide or make into our image. Our main responsibility is to share the "Good News" or gospel to those who are lost, and leave the changing part of ones life to God. For the church to awaken from its sleep we must show compassion with deeds worthy of respect, and be willing to listen to those we disagree with or disapprove of with an attitude of non-judgement. This is not an easy thing to do, but with God all things are possible for people of faith who trust Him. Please remember the words of a great founder of this nation, "the government of this nation will be blessed only to the extent that God fearing and morale individuals are placed into office." {Benjamin Rush}. Friends, our best opportunity for this to happen is for Christians to vote, and to vote responsibly.

ENLIGHTENMENT

Sometimes I am curious to know how various governments organize themselves often with good intentions but somehow they become corrupted by the human element. If just one leader becomes corrupted by greed and power, then thousands or millions of people suffer. I look to the Old Testament in the book of I Kings and II Kings and find lists of kings who ruled Israel and if the king was characterized as an evil king the kingdom suffered or was dominated by another ruler, and if the king was characterized as one who "did what was right" in the eyes of the Lord then the kingdom was never dominated by another ruler. It did not mean the country did not go through difficult times, and sometimes the king had made mistakes, but during the kings reign the kingdom was at rest with their enemies, and the people were content. This truth is reinforced in Psalms 67:4-5, "May the nations be glad and sing for joy, for you rule the peoples justly and guide the nations of the earth." Also in Proverbs chapter 8 the context of the writing is about "wisdom." In verses 13 thru 18 helps define what wisdom is; "To fear the Lord is to hate evil; I hate pride and arrogance, evil behavior and perverse speech. Counsel and sound judgment are mine; I have understanding and power. By me kings reign and rulers make laws that are just; by me princes govern, and all nobles who rule on earth. I love those who love me, and those who seek me find me." Obviously, this wisdom that is described in Proverbs is a choice. A king or ruler must seek for help from his maker, and if he does the people he rules over will rejoice and be content with his decision. However, if that king or ruler does not seek his creator, and decides to rule himself without God, then he opens the door to do evil, and the people mourn. This common theme runs true throughout the books of Kings. Rulers of the world's kingdoms need to do what is right for their people, but so often they do not. Even the Israelites who were ruled by kings were often given more wicked kings than righteous kings, but when the good kings reined they ruled for many years compared to the wicked kings.

I often think that our Founders were enlightened in their decisions on how they formed our Constitution and Declaration of Independence. They spoke of God and Jesus routinely in there writings and many of them were even involved in ministries through their various churches. The kind of government they searched for was tempered with checks and balances because they were fearful of any branch becoming too powerful. It almost seemed they understood how weak human rulers could be, and wanted as many counsels as possible to guide decisions that would fairly and justly represent the will of the people. They also gave careful thought to the rights of individual states, as they promoted local governments and state representatives.

Turning the page forward to Nazi Germany to a different kind of government is another story of failed policies of the past. Their government is best described as National Socialism that actually led to a dictatorship. It was terribly efficient because there is only one decision maker, and very few middle men. Adolf Hitler proved to be this kind of dictator. He was very charismatic speaker and he helped raise the people's hopes with his grand promises, as he popularized his ideas through community organizing. Once they gained the trust of the people through large crowds and rallies, the radical change was not far away. They did away with powerful influences such as the church, and virtually anyone who challenged their ideology. Once the national socialist party gained its power it actually spurred the economy with all the push towards military/arms build-up. They took over corporations, banks, and virtually stopped all businesses, especially in destroying the Hebrew community. But the people lost their soul when they gave up everything for the fanatical dreams of a dictator. As history provides us evidence of a light that burned brightly, but quickly died out. This ruler did not do what was right before his maker, and the people and the world suffered because of it. Remember, the only righteous king this world will eventually see, is Jesus.

We, the American people need to choose righteousness, not evil. We have for too long been complicit with wrong decisions coming from the wrong kind of leaders. If they do not humble themselves and seek their creator in their decisions we only end up with their narcissistic dreams of power and greed. Sometimes the grand ideals of government sound so wonderful, but after the glitter of pomp and circumstance, reality sets in and the great promises fall short of reality, deflated and hallow. Politicians promise the world, and you end up disappointed, if you're lucky. Still, I believe we have the best designed government this world has seen, and still people from all over the world long to come here. But a government no matter how well designed cannot operate when people are so fiercely divided. And, the reason they are divided is because we have organizational forces who are promoting a socialist revolution. And, we have elected officials who are operating as drones controlled by special interest groups who want to throw God and Christianity out the door. People really do not know who to trust in all the political bickering and we really need to study our Constitution, the original document! Not a book about the Constitution, because then you get a biased opinion which may or may not be represented in truth. You would do well to also read about the Founders of our nation, and what they wrote and what they envisioned in establishing this nation. Then become active in your community and promote a candidate who best represents the Constitution and your values.

RENEWING OUR FIRST LOVE

How does a nation renew its first love for God? Prophets of old often warned of impending doom if a nation did not turn back to God in repentance. Most of the time the nations did not heed the prophets warning and great suffering followed. On a few occasions they did listen to the prophet, and the nation was sparred. The gentile nation of Nineveh was revived when the king repented in sackcloth and his people did the same, staying God's judgment after heeding Jonah's warning. Repentance actually means a change in direction, or turn-around. I believe this is a requirement for nation leaders, as well a requirement for individuals. In the book of Isaiah: God says; "Come now, let us reason this out, "says the Lord." "No matter how deep the stain of your sins, I can remove it. I can make you as clean as freshly fallen snow. Even if you are stained as red as crimson, I can make you as white wool. If you will only obey me and let me help you, then you will have plenty to eat. But if you keep turning away and refusing to listen, you will be destroyed by your enemies. I the Lord, have spoken." Isaiah 1:18-20.

SPECIAL THANKS

I was strongly motivated by the writings of David Barton, author of the book "Original Intent." I must admit that up to that point I was terribly naïve of our nation's great history, and the great men (forefathers) who administered and framed our Constitution. Some of my writings are direct quotes from our Founders, and I am in complete agreement with David Barton's view on revisionists who so commonly make the mistake of regurgitating the words of others instead of citing the Founders own words. As consequence, many historians misinterpret the truest intent of our Founders meaning and words. I sincerely hope that David Barton will forgive me for using his book to motivate me to write one, and I must say I was largely ignorant of many American historical facts, and I am not a historian. Just want to be clear on that fact. But I am a concerned citizen who wants to inform others who may be standing in that sea of ignorance. Anyway, thank you David Barton for all your diligent work and service, and helping me see the great policies of the past, from great men who loved God and true freedom.

I want to offer special thanks to the authors of "Israel My Glory" magazine. They have especially enlightened me to a better understanding of God's chosen people and nation, and how they fit into God's miraculous plan today and in the future. Yes, you have inspired me to write and inform the American people to continue to pray for the peace of Jerusalem, and to act in support of Israel. God promises to bless America if we stand with Israel. I am so thankful that God led me to your wonderful writings, and you're spreading the truth of God's word (Bible) to all people who love God, both Jew and Gentile.

AUTHOR FORWARD

The intent of this writing is a peaceful protest of government intrusion in our lives, and in no way would be misconstrued or understood as a way to justify violence. I wholeheartedly encourage all people whether secular or religious to abstain from all thoughts or actions that would disrupt a peaceful society. As a Christian I am fully aware of my responsibility to be subject to the governing authorities. I also concur with Jesus' words to "Render to Caesar the things that are Caesar's, and to God the things that are God's;" (Mark 12:17). I realize I must give respect and allegiance to both kingdoms, God's kingdom and man's kingdom. Again, this is a peaceful and thought provoking writing written for the purpose of protecting the interest of others, both secular and religious in order to maintain a higher sense of justice. Our mission as Christians is to influence society and not to control it, as I realize we do live in a fallen world. Until we see Jesus establish his visible kingdom, our responsibility is to pray and try as we must to influence our society by being active in public service or in other areas whereas God has called us, for the goal of advancing the better good for all Americans.

"I exhort first of all that supplications, prayers, intercessions, and giving of thanks be made for all men, for kings and all who are in authority, that we may lead a quiet and peaceable life in all godliness and reverence. For this is good and acceptable in the sight of God our Savior, who desires all men to be saved and to come to the knowledge of the truth:" (1 Timothy 2:1-4).

WHY THE BOOK?

"*D*reams From Our Fathers" book was first published in 2012. So now in 2024, I have re-edited my book, hoping to help citizens see the massive efforts by President Biden and democrat politicians to push forward President Obama's dream to "fundamentally transform America." This unholy alliance to socialism and Marxism ideology and burdensome policies will eventually undo our freedoms in America.

This writing is an attempt to explain our government's greed and takeover of everything. The failed policies of the past is a reminder of Obama's own words and what his administration is attempting to do is really nothing new, has been tried before, and is doomed to failure. I will attempt to link true failures of past history in governments and human nature to what we are faced with in today's leadership in America. Hopefully, this book will give light to citizens as to how we over time have succumbed to lies and propaganda coming from leftist politicians, radical groups, liberal media fronts, activist judges, secular education, and liberal professors who have successfully infiltrated our culture, our youth, and our value system. Promoting an elitist and politically correct attitude and devious plan to overthrow our government and destroy our sovereignty as a nation. Attempting to subvert our Constitution and remove our time tested Judeo-Christian belief system, and faith in a personal and loving God.

As common folks who trust in traditional beliefs really need to be active in any way we can to fight the secularist invasion and most importantly walk with God. We need to help our younger generation to understand the dangers of national socialism/communism and atheistic movements who have become engrained in our government and public educational system. We must come together, no matter what political party persuasion and look beyond our differences, and unite in opposition to those who want to change our form of government, and lead us away from a trust and faith in God. We are in fact fighting for truth and for God, and if we are faithful to his calling, he will fight for us.

Do not think I am advocating a religious government or monarchy of any kind, because I believe our founding fathers had it right when they created "a government of the people, for the people, and by the people" and a government of checks and balances, and who in fact were men of Christian faith who trusted in the Holy Scriptures to give them guidance. But today our leaders and society has drifted away from these time tested values. We now act on a deistic morality and do things on our own and not truly acting in faith, but relying solely on our own wisdom. Some have drifted away from faith into atheistic movements and belief systems of humanism. Why are we as a country struggling so much with debt issues and character issues among our politicians and leaders? They have not been taught the difference between right and wrong and were taught to believe that moral absolutes are a myth. We fail to recognize who we are, and we lack faith, and we fail to do what is right and ethical as we once did as a culture and nation.

These writings were put together over the past couple of years as expressions of my dismay at the direction of our nation is heading, and the actions of government officials and explaining why they do what they do. I have no special talent in writing, but this effort is something that average folks can read and understand coming from someone who is quite common with humble beginnings. Thank you for reading my book, and may our great God give you comfort and guidance for the future, and boldness to do what you can do to preserve our freedoms and preserve our founders vision for America.

I am thankful for conservative radio voices coming from Glen Beck, Rush Limbaugh, Mark Levin, Sean Hannity, Mike Savage and so many others not mentioned who have been successful in warning many of us of all the corruption and dangers of a growing government. These great voices have truly inspired Americans towards enlightenment and activism that took root in the "Tea Party," an independent movement of Constitutional Conservatives to rally America back to our historical roots. Pray for them, and support them, and remember they are not perfect men without flaws but are men who have great passion who dearly love our country. They need our encouragement and support. May their diligence and love for our country be a reflection of our great creator, and may they inspire other great men and women to be involved in government that will hopefully lead us back to freedom.

This writing is based on five presuppositions:

*Many former Presidents believed and trusted in God, and because of their reliance on God their leadership was used to bless and prosper our nation.

*There is no evidence that socialism and Marxist thought has blessed or prospered our nation since these movements invaded our nation in the early 1900's, but has done much to divide us in ideology, and cripple us economically.

*Our Constitution and Declaration of Independence are great documents, and our elected officials and appointed judges must be held accountable to the oath they took to uphold these guided principles as intended by our forefathers.

*Citizens must remember that our founding father writings supported Judeo-Christian values and morality that have served us well in American history, and we should not forget their great faith. We would do well to express our faith in preserving these intrinsic freedoms as endowed by our creator.

*Our past support for the nation Israel should not be abandoned, because blessing or curse is God's solemn promise, and He will keep it. We are at the crossroads.

CHAPTER 1

HUMBLE BEGINNINGS

This book is written for common folks with no special notoriety or privilege. People who work hard, love their families, and love the freedom our country stands for, and never forgets the sacrifice of patriots who fought and died to preserve the inherent God given right to life and liberty. Do not be offended by the word "Common." Average folks usually have the good sense to know what is right and what is wrong, and the dignity to discern what is honest and true, and I dare say could solve our nation's woes if we had a responsive government who would listen. If only the "Common" would unite together for the cause of freedom and remember our nation's beginnings, instead of being manipulated by government and politics. Our countries roots comes from pilgrims, some aristocrats and some nobility, but mostly poor hard working people of faith who yearned for individual dignity and a place they could call home. They were all united on one front; freedom. Free from oppressive governments and state controlled churches, and people of power who controlled their lively-hood and manipulated them into slavery. Never think that you are a lesser person than the elites who have enormous sums of money or power because every person was made by the same lump of clay. Some are endowed with greater gifts to help others, and if they do not, they will incur a stricter judgment when they stand before their creator. All persons are created equal and made in God's image and are a reflection of him, but no man will boast before God, but all will bow before him. This great God is not an earthly king with temporary powers, but an eternal king.

I for one believe America was once God's country, but I fear there is a growing majority teetering on total rejection of God, and Christianity in particular. We can learn from history if we choose to; thus we need to be reminded of our humble beginnings. Are we so quick to forget our miraculous victory over Britain, our great Constitution formed by men of faith, a great president and man of faith who kept us together during the purging of our nation's sins in the civil war, and surviving and winning two world wars? How can anyone believe God was not with us in our struggles? America remains the most giving country this world has ever seen in protecting freedom, giving money, food, and giving comfort to those in need. We still produce missionaries and church helpers and medical aid to the poor of the world, and we promote another country's prosperity provided they are not hostile, and we do not conquer their lands. We still lead the world in demonstrating justice and compassion and some nations have followed our lead and remain our friends like England, Canada, Australia, Israel, and South Korea. We have allies who were once our enemies like Japan and Germany, and we have other European, South American and African nations, and island nations who look to us as a beacon light and freedom to the world.

Yet with all of America's great deeds, we must not forget our God and his faithfulness that leads men to repentance, recognizing a biblical truth that all men "are sinful and come short of the glory of God," (Romans 3:23 KJV). Godly sorrow actually honors God, and it is through this kind of humility and trust in God that man can be used for his glory. "Righteousness exalts a nation, but sin is a disgrace to any people," (Proverbs 14:34).

American Roots

God's vision for America was to be a beacon of light of freedom to protect individual rights and dignity. Foreign nations of the revolutionary period stood in awe at the growth and prosperity of America, and foreign nations are still inspired by what our nation has accomplished since its beginnings. It is not by accident that peoples from all over the world still desire to come to America. Even people of humble beginnings and background have opportunity to advance themselves in the land of freedom. The Bible teaches that our creator desires that his truth be spread to the four corners of the earth, and at the center of his goal is to preserve God given rights and to offer freedom of sin to every soul who seeks his truth. Jesus said, "I am the way, the truth, and the life, no man comes to the father except through me." This world is at war against this truth and the enemy is always at the door to misguide, to confuse, and to silence this truth. America is unique in that our founders were searching for a new home, free from oppressive kings and governments who regularly persecuted them for their faith. Our founders were mostly protestant reformers from various European and island nations. Their was fifty-six founders who signed the Declaration of Independence who exerted influence and prominent leadership in establishing our nation as an independent and self-governing country. But, their were more than fifty-six founders. Many historians agree that others influenced the beginnings of America like Patrick Henry, Noah Webster, ninety members of Congress who created the Bill of Rights. Actually, there are some 250 individuals who are considered founding fathers. were they always in agreement? No, they were not always in agreement, but they were united in their passion for freedom. George Washington encountered all the bickering and debating from the forefathers in forming the Constitution, and he called for a recess for all to go home for three days and pray for God's wisdom. Our founders came from varying denominations like Congregational, Unitarian, Baptist, Presbyterian, Quaker, Episcopalian and other protestant churches. Some were also "deists" who believed in God, but not in terms of a personal relationship as much as most protestant churches asserted through the authoritative word of God. Deists were a small minority of that time, but what was important to remember that our founders were unified in their passion and purpose to preserve religious freedom and individual freedom given to them by God. They desired the free right to choose what they wanted to believe, and forming a government that was not controlled by a religious power, or one specific church, but a free people who had a right to express their faith and Christian convictions the way they felt lead by God. These men had a tremendous respect for the Holy Scriptures. These men were not atheists, nor were these men who believed in foreign religions because they were men unified in their commonality of their Christian faith, and their passion for liberty and freedom.

Much is spoken of just one of the twenty-seven grievances against Britain, "no taxes without representation." Many other grievances against Britain were listed such as anti-slavery laws, the will of the people, rights to a military, judicial injustice, moral issues and religious liberty. The top three grievances against Britain was their abuse of government powers, many states desired to abolish slavery, and the religious right to spread the gospel to Indian tribes. In 1774, Virginia created laws to abolish slavery, but King George vetoed the laws. Britain was steeped heavily in the slave trade of that time. Interestingly, George Washington desired an end to slavery even though he owned slaves on his property. Revisionists historians attempt to smear his reputation by spreading all kinds of untruths, because if they can re-write Washington's history, the revisionists can affect public policy in government. George Washington tried to abolish slavery in his own state, and he signed the first federal anti-slavery laws. But his state came up one vote short of abolishing slavery. Consequently, America allowed slavery to continue for another 120 years. George Washington has been much maligned for having slaves but history gives evidence that he treated them more like indentured servants and provided for them well and gave them property. He also recruited them in his continental army as one-fourth of his fighting force was Negro slaves who were granted freedom for their service. After Washington served as president and refusing to serve a second term he continued to provide for his servants and actually lost much of his property for support of his workers. Going forward in time, Revisionist historians became popular in the 1920's and re-focused a new secular view by atheists who started the "American Civil Liberties Union," and their main goal was to remove God from textbooks. As well, in the 1960's they dramatically changed from the religious moral teachings to an economic view thus completing a total change in how history is taught in schools. Now, they continue to malign our founding fathers into something less than complimentary. No wonder our youth do not learn the truth about our founding fathers and great presidents, unless of course that president happens to fit into their worldview. This is why the progressives try to reenact the policies of the past from presidents who believed in big government more than they believed in protecting God given freedoms. These presidents they admonished were Franklin D. Roosevelt and Woodrow Wilson. Interestingly, both these presidents were responsible for creating the terrible depression, and for prolonging the depression. In my opinion, if it were not for WWII which spurred the economy, America might still be suffering from that depression period. But, as it stands today, we have an administration that is intentionally putting us into immense debt, and trying to create a depression so as to create opportunity or crisis if you will, so Americans will become more willing to accept socialism/communism as a new kind of government and worldview.

Today, we have a president who happens to fit that very worldview. A view that believes in big government and a view that eliminates the Judeo-Christian God and promotes a humanistic and secular government that will impose harmful influence in our society. Our current administration have taken astonishing positions such as support of abortion, gay rights, and a new openness towards Islam and a promoting of a growing government who is actually taken over failing corporations and banks. Our nation has morally failed, supporting sexual decadence, socialistic economics and anti-Christian ideas of governance. Our forefathers were so much different on their views. During the American Revolution John Adams wrote to Thomas Jefferson reflecting on the sacrifices of men and women for the cause of freedom. John Adams said, "that army of young fellows" had all been bound together lay two critical ideas: First, they had been educated in the general principles of Christianity." Second, they had been educated in the "principles of English and American Liberty." These two concepts of liberty and Christianity cannot be separated. Our government is also slipping away from national sovereignty. In Acts 17:36 we have evidence that God intentionally created nations and their boundaries. In Genesis 11:6 more documented evidence explains how and why the Lord opposed ideas of a single, unified global government. God is clear on what is morally right and wrong. We have the Ten Commandments, and we have clear instruction on the value of human life all throughout the Holy Scriptures and all of mankind is created in our creator's image. We must never forget what the Bible says, and what our Declaration of Independence teaches us when our forefathers said; "We hold these truths to be self-evident, that all men are created equal, that they are endowed by their Creator with certain unalienable Rights, that among these are Life, Liberty and the pursuit of Happiness." But when governmental mandates collide with the Declaration of Independence and God's instruction manual on matters of life and liberty, we must stand together against such ungodly mandates.

Re-Visit Our Founders

Revisionist historians do great harm in distorting American history by making bold assertions, taking words totally out of context, and often miss-quoting our Founding fathers. For example they often assert that Adams and Jefferson were atheists. So, one must go to the original documents of what they actually said and wrote down on paper. In Adams writings to Jefferson he said, "That it would be fanatical to desire a world without religion, for such a world would be hell." Jefferson wrote back and declared that "he agreed." Critics also quote Washington's words during the "Barbary Powers Conflict," when he said "the United

States is in no sense founded on the Christian religion" in the 1797 Treaty of Tripoli. To give context to his statement, Muslim pirates captured American ships and enslaved Christian seaman in retaliation of centuries of conflict that occurred in the "Crusade Holy Wars." To avoid any miss-understanding Article XI was created during Adams presidency explaining that America had no desire for another "Holy War" or any hatred towards Muslim countries. Therefore, if the article is read as a declaration that the federal government of the United States was not in any sense founded on the Christian religion, such a statement is not a repudiation of the fact that America was highly influenced by Christian principles and values. The United States was not ruled by a state church. The European crusaders were controlled by a state church. Interestingly, the Muslim religion dominated in governmental affairs much like European crusaders were dominated by the universal Christian church in Rome. Article XI simply distinguishes America from the hateful crusades motivated by European Christianity who was caught up in hatred for Muslims. President Adams did not want America to be lumped into a band of Christianity like those of previous nations in Europe. Noah Webster supported this fact in his writings, and supported that "America's Christianity was tolerant and peaceful and not motivated by hate."

In Adam's own words he declared: "The general principles on which that fathers achieved independence were.....the general principles of Christianity....I will avow that I then believed, and now believe, that those general principles of Christianity are as eternal and immutable as the existence and attributes of God; and that those principles of liberty are as unalterable as human nature."

To secure the peace between the United States and Muslim nations, Eaton, commander of the warship "Hero" wrote a letter to Pickering of how pleased a Barbary ruler had been when he received compensations from America in the treaties. He said, "To speak truly and candidly..... we must acknowledge to you that we have never received articles of the kind of so excellent a quality from any Christian nation."

Interestingly, numerous religions did exist in America at the time of the Founders, and that there was value to society from varying faiths, but they were clear in their preference of the Christian faith. In John Adams letter to Thomas Jefferson he said: "Who composed that army of young fellows that was then before my eyes? There were among them Roman Catholics, English Episcopalians, Scotch and American Presbyterians, Methodists, Moravians, Anabaptists, German Lutherans, German Calvinists, Universalists, Arians, Priestleyans, Socinians, Independents, Congregationalists, Horse Protestants, and House Protestants, Deists, and Atheists, and Protestants "qui ne croyent reign." Very few, however, of several of these species: nonetheless, all educated in the general principles of Christianity......" Today we describe the "general principles of Christianity" as the "Judeo-Christian Ethic." The Founders showed a great respect to the "Hebrews," but nonetheless they believed that the teachings of Christ provided the greatest benefit for civil society. Evident by what Thomas Jefferson said, "The precepts of philosophy, and of the Hebrew code, laid hold of actions only. He (Jesus) pushed his scrutinies into the heart of man; erected his tribunal in the region of his thoughts, and purified the waters at the fountain head."

The Constitutional prohibition against "an establishment of religion" forbade only the federal establishment of a national denomination. Charles Carroll (a Roman Catholic) the only Catholic to sign the Declaration of Independence said "the only reason that he and many other Founders had entered the Revolution was to ensure that all Christian denominations were place on equal footing."

Anti-Federalists Vision and Warnings

In the federal convention of 1787 Benjamin Franklin gave us his thoughts concerning his opposition to executive salaries. He said, "There are two passions which have a powerful influence on the affairs of men. These are ambitions and avarice; the love of power, and the love of money." He stressed that "politicians go to a post of honor, not a place of profit, and that these things were in fact affecting the British government." The anti-federalists, which of whom Mr. Franklin was, and nearly half of our founding fathers were very concerned about certain aspects of the Constitution's forming. The anti-federalists goal for the American Revolution which also included famous founding fathers, Patrick Henry, Pinckney, Wilson, Rutledge, Sherman, Gerry, and Randolph debated strenuously on the issue of executive powers. They certainly were cautious of ever being ruled by a tyrannical king, and their vision for America and the passion of their views did greatly affect the writing of our Constitution. They had a positive idealism of a "small, pastoral republic where virtuous, self-reliant citizens managed their own affairs and shunned the power and glory of an empire." To them, their victory in the Revolutionary War was not meant to make America a world power, but a "genuine republican polity, far from greed, lust of power, and tyranny." They cherished emphasis on states and local councils and committees and Articles of Confederation where the central government rested entirely on the states, where the representatives really knew their people in their districts, and listened to their concerns. Benjamin Franklin also warned that "the more the people are discontented with the oppression of taxes, the greater need the prince has of money to distribute among his partisans and pay the troops that are to suppress all resistance, and enable him to plunder at pleasure!" Franklin also gave us examples of Pharaoh: "get first all the peoples money, then all their lands, and then make them and their children servants forever." Franklin certainly expressed apprehension that the government of these states may in future times, end in a monarchy!

The anti-federalists goal of the American Revolution was to end the lure of world dominance where depraved rulers exacted subservience and a gradual erosion of human decency and virtue of the people. They warned of commercial growth, westward expansion, increased national power and world diplomacy. They felt these endeavors would eventually lead into dangerous ideas of consolidated government and universal empire. Something that the American Revolution had been fought to eradicate. They wanted to keep America a sovereign nation, so as to keep the sacred freedoms of speech and preserve and protect their beloved Christian religion. They struggled a lot in their concerns to balance power, and were especially concerned about the powers of the judiciary, which they believed had little protection in preserving "checks and balances" in government. As well, they were concerned about the powers of Congress to enact unjust taxes and ignore the will of the people. The anti-federalists desired a small government whose sole purpose was to unite the states for a militia for the protection of our country in case of war. No other purpose was desired for the government.

How far we have drifted from the will and desire of our great fathers? Did they not do great diligence in warning us? Did they not give us great examples of self sacrifice? But we have forgotten our father's great words and have chosen to be plagued with activist judges who ignore our founding fathers intentions and ignore our Constitution so they can make-up their own laws. How convenient and how treasonous! Today we see the corruption of power and the love of money permeated throughout government that has most defiantly affected both political parties. I have mentioned this before, but it cannot be stated enough the great words of our first president, "excessive allegiance to one political party will lead to corruption." In my optimistic view, all we have to do is vote for the right person who best honors our great Constitution, honors God, honors the family institution, and is free from the "love of money." I know, this sounds impossible, but if you look closely at the people your voting for you may find that virtuous person. Your children are counting on you to vote responsibly.

British Elitism

Because of King George and British Parliament decisions to enact unjust laws that eventually led to murder, and by treating the colonist as less than equal is what led to the Boston Massacre, and eventually to the Revolutionary War. The violent act at Boston led to a brewing discontent the colonists felt because of the Townshend Acts which gave government intrusion into colonist's homes securing their property. Samuel Adam's and his followers called "Sons of Liberty" preferred boycotting the British authoritative power and governments intrusion, but John Dickenson preferred to use his pen to voice his opposition. He recognized God's supreme authority and includes prayers in his many letters to King George and Parliament. His prayer quote was: "But above all, let us implore the protection of that infinite good and gracious being, by whom Kings reign and princes decree justice." He was recognized as "A Farmer in Pennsylvania," and later earned him the name "Penman of the Revolution." He did all he could be loyal to British rule, and his respectful letters were obvious to all.

Reverend Samuel Cooke addressed the growing tensions by a tempered approach. He reminded his audiences that the Supreme Ruler "allows and approves of the establishment of government among men." Cooke reminded the British that they had a responsibility to make understandable laws and that purposefully confusing the uneducated man was immoral and deceitful. He said, "Fidelity to the public requires that the laws be as plain and explicit as possible, that the less knowing may understand, and not be ensnared by them, while the artful evade their force." He believed government was not for the elite alone, but for the protection of the weak as well. He said, "The benefits of the Constitution and the laws must extend to every branch and each individual in society, of whatever degree, that every man may enjoy his property." Cooke urged British rulers to lead by example. He said, "Rulers are appointed guardians of the Constitution in their respective stations, and must confine themselves within the limits by which their authority is circumscribed." Cooke also reminded the British that when mistakes were made it would be best to acknowledge their failure to the people. He said, "Justice also requires of rulers, in their legislative capacity, that they attend to the operation of their own acts and repeal whatever laws, upon an impartial review, they find to be inconsistent with the laws of God, the right of men, and the general benefit of society." Basically, leaders today need to stop the political expediency and outright lies just to benefit their party power. But sadly today many prefer their party over the will of the people, and lack integrity to do what is right.

The purpose of sharing the writings of Dickenson and Reverend Samuel Cooke was to help understand their integrity and efforts to abide in peaceful protest, but their efforts were ignored by the elites in British government. This same kind of elitism is being demonstrated in today's government. As God's ambassadors, we need to stand up peacefully to a growing and intrusive government, and to do all we can to ensure a better government led by men and women of moral character and integrity.

Divine Rights of Kings

The Constitution is the most precious document that must be preserved, unaltered and protected from those advocating ignoring it or outright subverting it in order to establish a national socialist government. We must not forget our founders who gave a great sacrifice to provide a government that is not oppressive to its people. We dare not forget their Christian convictions and original thinking in providing a government of the people, by the people and for the people. As I see it the most fundamental thing we must do is reignite our first love of freedom. Our founders showed us a great light and path to follow and we must go back to our history and discover who we really are as children of great fathers who cherished freedom. It will be difficult to rekindle the fire and passion of our forefathers but what made them united was the great suffering they encountered from the hands of an oppressive monarchy government that infringed on God-given rights. They no longer believed in the "Divine Rights of Kings" but united around the truth that only our creator God was worthy of worship. Consequently, they gave God pre-eminence in their lives and they trusted him to give them courage, strength, and insight to fight the physical and spiritual battle that was facing them. They overcame great odds in defeating the world's greatest army of that period, and they gave God credit for that victory. This thankfulness and recognition of God's intervention in their affairs is clearly evident in their writings. God and freedom cannot be separated and they earnestly believed they were one of the same. All of the chains that bind us from experiencing God inspired freedoms are the results of man's attempt to run government apart from God. The result of such prideful thinking has pushed us headlong into disastrous policies.

As we look back to the Revolutionary period, exactly how were the rights of a free people infringed? John Adams wrote in the Declaration of Independence what the British monarchy was doing.

Quotes:
- Relinquish the right of representation in legislature
- Compliance with his (King George III) measures
- Dissolved representative Houses. "Rights of the people"
- Exposed to dangers of invasion
- Prevented the population of these States
- Obstructed the laws of naturalization of foreigners
- Obstructed the administration of justice....refusing... establishment of Judiciary powers
- Made judges dependant on his will alone (King George III)
- Swarms of officers to harass our people
- Standing armies without the consent of our legislature
- Render the military independent of and superior to civil power
- Subject us to a jurisdiction foreign to our Constitution
- Quartering large bodies of armed troops among us
- Protecting (troops), by a mock trial, from punishment for any murders
- Cutting off trade with all parts of the world
- Imposing taxes on us without consent
- Depriving us in many cases of the benefits of trial by jury
- Transporting us (colonists) beyond seas to be tried for pretended offenses

- Abolishing the free system of English laws...."establishment therein an arbitrary government" leading to "absolute rule into these Colonies"
- For taking away our charters, abolishing our most valuable laws....
- Out of his protection and waging war against us
- Plundered our sea's, ravaged our coasts, burnt our towns, destroyed the lives of our people
- He is at the time transporting large armies of foreign mercenaries
- Constrained our fellow citizens captive on the high seas to bear arms against their country
- Excited domestic insurrections among us.... (Indian warfare)

We can see from Adam's writings that what King George III did is similar in some ways to what President Obama is doing today, not entirely, but in part. I believe he (President Obama) is at war with our Declaration of Independence and Constitution, and although he wouldn't admit it, his actions speak volumes. Therefore we must judge him according to what he has done. It is clear to me that he is crippling us into immense debt and promoting social policies that attack our God given freedoms to live free, and the promotion of burdensome and excessive taxes. If you look back at the list of crimes Britain enforced on the colonies, some might conclude our President's administration is doing similar things. As his power grows more, the right of a free people will be less. In his inaugural address on April 13th he made statements that eluded to his belief that what made America great occurred in 1965, adding social programs of Medicaid and Medicare and social security enacted under President Roosevelt in 1945.

To boastfully proclaim that these social programs made America great is a blatant disrespect to our forefathers for what they suffered and endured and ignoring the fact that if it were not for these great men we would not know freedom in America as we now know it!

Just War Theory

The "Just War Theory" has a long history dating back to the ancient Greeks and Romans. Our forefathers had great respect for Christian philosophers of that period from such men as Augustine and Thomas Aquinas who had a strong influence on the development of the "Just War Theory." The words of Augustine were as follows: "True religion looks upon as peaceful those wars that are waged not for motives of aggrandizement, or cruelty, but with the object of securing peace, of punishing evil-doers, and of uplifting the good." I think our founders has this in mind when they decided to revolt against England that led to the War of Independence.

Sometimes people are divided on what is a just cause to go to war against a government or nation. Some think that there is never a good reason to go to war. They would be called "pacifists." On September 27, 1938 Neville Chamberlain, Prime Minister of England felt the need to negotiate with Adolf Hitler in the Munich Treaty. This kind of appeasement endangered the survival of Great Britain. In the "limited liability" doctrine, the British Army suffered massive cuts. Prime Minister Chamberlain did however support the RAF and Navy, but he was opposed by the Labour Party (equivalent to our present liberal politics), which always voted against a defense budget. Possibly it would be unfair to label Chamberlain as a pacifist, but he certainly was very reluctant to go to war, and certainly naïve to think that he could negotiate with a terrorist. If it were not for the United States entering the war and supporting with arms and supplies, Great Britain would have fallen to defeat under Nazi Germany. The great lesson to be learned is that Great Britain could have been more prepared for war, and to never negotiate with murderers and nation leaders who are motivated by evil motives. As well, never should a country or countrymen be quick to go to war, but wise leaders of great nations will always be prepared before the need arises. It should be noted that England was not alone in not being prepared, because clearly the United States was not fully prepared for war, nor did our leaders take the threat seriously enough.

I think it is fair to say that if an enemy threatens a good and peaceful society, then war becomes the only means (unless God intervenes), to regain civility and peace.

Sabbath Rest, Natural Blessings

The early colonists were always extolling the virtues of "natural rights." They believed natural rights were "God given." Reverend Simon Howard a respected pastor of the colonial period spoke often on scripture in Galatians 5:1, "stand therefore in the liberty wherewith Christ hath made you free" (KJV). In explaining the context of the verse Howard explained the conflict between Jewish and Gentile Christians on whether they should follow Jewish ceremonial laws. The Apostle Paul explained that Christ had given them liberty by setting them free from the law. Howard believed in this freedom when he defined natural rights as "everything that is opposed to the temporal slavery." Or "all those advantages which are liable to be destroyed by the art or power of men." He also believed natural liberty had limits when he said "This however is not a state of licentiousness, for the law of nature which bounds this liberty, forbids all injustice and wickedness; allows no man to injure another in his person or property or to destroy his own life." In short, he believed government's responsibility was to respect and protect those God given rights and freedoms; and that the blessings of God were governed by him. Howard's preaching expressed the point that the resurrected Christ as "the head of God's providential government."

If we say we believe in God our worth is not determined by any man-made law or evaluation, it is based solely on the truth that we are all made in the image of God, (Gen. 1:27). God looks to the heart; and by creating men and women in his image, he gave the natural blessings of intrinsic worth.

CHAPTER 2

CONSTITUTIONAL CRIME

Our founding fathers faith in God was best expressed in the Declaration of Independence. "We hold these truths to be self-evident, that all men are created equal, that they are endowed by their Creator with certain unalienable Rights that among these are Life, Liberty and the pursuit of Happiness." Today, we are surrounded by elected officials who do not believe this truth, and that's the problem. The "good book" or Bible is not revered and respected as it once was, and even though the Ten Commandments are boldly inscribed in the Supreme Court halls, even our Supreme Court judges fail to follow its dictates and parameters. Since, our elected and appointed officials no longer look to the Bible for truth and guidance; it is no wonder our leaders are drifting away from our founding Constitution. As citizens who believe that we are given inherent God given rights of freedom have we forgotten these words from the Declaration of Independence? "That to secure these rights, Governments are instituted among Men, deriving their just powers from the consent of the governed, --That whenever any Form of Government becomes destructive of these ends, it is the Right of the People to alter or to abolish it, and to institute new Government." Would it not be interesting if some kind of Constitutional crime bill be passed and enforced when politicians and judges are found acting aggressively towards subverting or changing our Constitution? Previous presidents and our present administration are currently ignoring our Constitution. One example is this, nothing in the Constitution grants or guarantees health care. Another example of blatantly ignoring the law and Constitution is to allow illegal aliens access through our borders, especially from Mexico where millions enter every year. And, to compound the problem our administration wants to give free health care to illegal's. Another clear breaking of Constitutional law is an old ruling of the 1940's of "separation of church and state." Allowing the atheists to promote all kinds of ridiculous laws in our society promoted by liberal judges and politicians and influences from the ACLU and other radical organizations, and the blatant indoctrination in our schools telling our youth what to think instead of how to think is at the root of our countries problems. Hamilton's quote of saying "separation of church and state" is clearly intended to mean that the United States would not be ruled by a church power or any one denominational church. Our founders were sensitive of being ruled by foreign power or church, and because their descendants came from Europe where they were persecuted for their protestant faith by the universal Church of Rome, and the Church of England. Hamilton's quote is taken entirely out of context by our present court system, and fail to look at true intent of documented history.

Our Constitution was formed to create checks and balances where no one entity or group would have absolute power, because even kids being bullied understand this principle. It has been quoted many times, but still people don't listen. "Absolute power corrupts absolutely!" That is why we have a Congress, a Senate, a House of Representatives, county courts, state courts, and federal courts, local governments, vice presidents and presidents. As well, we have a Constitution that is clear in its intended meaning and not thousands of pages in length, about 10 pages. Why do people in our courts constantly debate what is Constitutional or not. It is not because they do not understand it, they do not agree with it, and that is why we have people like Al Gore saying "the Constitution is a living and breathing document!" In other words, a convenient way to alter, change, or add to the Constitution the way he would like it, you know, wild theories of global warming would certainly be in the Constitution. Call me crazy, but I think some kind of Constitutional law testing be required for all public officials, and if they are found to be outside the boundaries of our country's laws, then they should be removed from office. Another way to ensure integrity would be to enforce term limits. As it has been said many times, we have too many career politicians and have been corrupted by political powers and special interests. George Washington gave America a beautiful example of how a president should act when he refused a second term. One of his quotes was this; "excessive allegiance to any one political party will lead to excessive political corruption." But the problem we have today is not very many politicians have that kind of character, and are more bent on their power, and it doesn't matter if they lie or cheat to get there, because they actually believe just reaching the goal by any means. Their philosophy is inspired by communism that believes in the collective and not the individual, or better understood as "the end justifies the means." This is not what we need in America, we need men and women of character who live by the truth, uphold the truest intents of the Constitution, and will honorably represent the people.

Truly, any honest investigation of what our founding fathers believed is clearly documented. They believed in a personal God written about in the Holy Scriptures. Any other false religion or notion was not supported. They were men who tolerated other denominations and beliefs and did not want a repeat of the disastrous war of the crusades, but neither did they want a government to control or influence various Christian convictions. No evidence is their that they wanted a theocracy, but they dearly believed in freedom for the individual and desired a small government whose main reason for existence was to provide a standing army and navy to protect us from foreign invaders.

It all comes down to this, that our Constitution ought not to be re-written by atheists. Removing God from our founding documents, removing him from our schools, removing him from our culture, or removing him from our government equals disaster. It is like taking the heart and soul out of our reason for existence, and it certainly takes the heart out of our Constitution. Our government and our public schools have gone astray with notions that worship of a biblical God is outdated and foolish. Interestingly, the Bible makes it clear, "that only the fool says there is no God" (KJV), and "that the beginning of wisdom is to fear God and keep his commandments" (KJV). Our country is experiencing the beginning of woes and catastrophes, and things will not get better by trusting only in failed human policies of the past. Look to history of a nation who went the way of National Socialism, and a charismatic leader. The nation was Nazi Germany, and the man was Hitler. Look to totalitarianism and communism and what does history teach you? You have Stalin and Lenin who were the leaders of communist Russia, and responsible for millions of murders within their own country. Look at Pol Pot, communist leader famous for the "killing fields," and yes he was responsible for millions of murders. Look at Mao, once a communist leader of China, and again he was responsible for millions of murders. Look to Edi Amine in Africa, communist leader, responsible for brutal murders of Christians. Get the picture? Yet we have tolerated communist and socialist teachers in our universities for years, and they indoctrinate our youth constantly, and we stand back and do nothing. And now we are faced with communist and socialist government, and radical leaders who are leading us down a very destructive path, and we don't vote! For those who do vote I am not talking to you, but we have so many people who are apathetic or don't care where our nation is heading, and I truly fear for our youth and our country. History gives us a clear picture of nations who trusted powerful leaders and tyrannical kings, and yes communist/socialist leaders who murdered millions of people who wanted freedom, and these leaders did all this murdering for the sake of their selfish vision of glory and authoritative power!

The two great commandments in Exodus and in the gospels is that we should "love God with all of our heart, and we should love our neighbor as much as we love ourselves," and is at the very crux of our existence and meaning of life. When any nation chooses to worship a man-made power or idol they are doomed to fail, and repeat the mistakes of the past. The Constitution should not critiqued as an outdated document because its guidance has given us prosperity and blessing, and even though we have had failures along the way which threatened our existence, God did not abandon us. Why should we abandon our faith in God now? We somehow think we are more enlightened that our forefathers. I think not. Technology has certainly progressed, but the condition of the human heart has not improved because man is still rebellious towards God will, and man is still selfish, greedy, malicious and capable of hate. Only through God's redemptive power can we change into a person God wants us to be, through his Son, and only through God's enlightened book can we see light to follow his path, and his purpose for our life.

Wisdom's Beginning

Proverbs 1:7 states that the "fear of the Lord is the beginning of knowledge; but fools despise wisdom and instruction." The next verse encourages a son to hear the instruction of a father, and not to forsake the law of a mother. The good book gives us a simple outline and order of things to follow to guide us to a right path, but today's misguided leaders have forgotten the inspired words, or chose not to live by them. The only un-inspired words from a flawed morality code we seem to adopt nowadays are things like political correctness, cultural awareness and diversity, tolerance for alternative lifestyles, and questionable rights for those who don't deserve it whether they be aliens or terrorists. Then we always seem to tolerate the ACLU's drumbeat of separation of church and state, and their obsession to take away citizens civil rights and offer it to radical groups. Then we tolerate activist judges who attempt with a flawed wisdom to trump the people's will with what seems to be logical to them, ignoring existing laws, and a bold re-writing of our Constitutional freedoms. In short, our government is attempting to take away our fundamental and foundational freedoms of free speech, religion, and rights to own property. Activist college professors continue to brainwash our youth with socialist propaganda, and the lie of moral relativism. Sadly, few of our youth ever challenge these presuppositional views of humanism and socialism. Much of the curriculum in the humanities field is permeated with social coursework. Code phrases of social justice, social economics, and many other phrases are used commonly and confused with human compassion. Socialism promotes government control but is cleverly intertwined with human compassion. Human compassion comes from an individual's choice, and never mandated by a government. Socialist leaders never abide by the same rules as forced upon the masses, thus they expect special treatment as someone who is elite or god-like. This is why many socialist and communist leaders demand obedience to their decisions, and always have large and bold banners with their faces on it, but never will they support an individuals rights to liberty and freedom. This is humanism in its purest form, replacing God with a human leader. Have you ever asked yourself why public schools and institutions prevent teachers of the Judeo-Christian faith from giving an argument or apologetic to secular humanist viewpoints, in fact there is no challenge at all! They constantly criticize the Christian faith as foolish, so they become successful in causing a vast misunderstanding or appreciation that the Christian faith is viable and reasonable. Have your ever wondered what these self-righteous know-it-alls are afraid of? They say they are afraid of a Christian take-over, but what they are really afraid of is losing their power and influence in the academic world. Again, it goes back to the early stages of the "progressive movement," because if they can change the history books and promote their socialist ideology in changing policies leading to their dream of a socialist government, they are happy. Even the unfair theory of evolution (Darwinism) is forced upon our youth from a very early age in all public schools. Taught as something that is scientifically proven, but it is not proven. It remains a theory. Our great educators who advocate their superior wisdom have chosen for us what is best to believe. Quite frankly, such elitist attitudes disgust me, and it is wrong that the silent majority are afraid to stand up for what they believe. This same kind of elitist attitude is permeating throughout our society evidenced by unjust and irrational laws of eminent domain, smoking bans, gun bans, environmental protective species bans that are in many cases are irrational and causing loss of personal liberty, loss of jobs and a loss of personal property. Elected officials are leaning more and more towards socialist practices imposing a belief system not dissimilar to a state religion. These self-righteous attitudes in federal, state, and local governments are wrong and not truly American. We are supposed to be a government represented by the people, and not ruled by an elitist monarchy of socialism. What is wrong with having a fair vote on any issue that affects the American citizen? Nothing of course, but we are not being fairly listened too, nor are we being represented like the Constitution mandates. This was evidenced in town-hall meetings with Congressmen who didn't like the public uproar over government healthcare. They received strong resistance, but they still insist on pushing the healthcare plan that they came up with, and rejecting any other ideas to alternative healthcare.

Should we not oppose public officials, educators, judges, politicians or any so-called civil rights group from telling the good citizens of America what we should do or shouldn't do? Let the people decide, and not a political party! Let the Constitutional laws abide, and let it rule. Our founding fathers envisioned a small government with freedoms for Judeo-Christian faiths to lighten our path towards truth, but not to force it on anyone, especially one particular faith. This is what the Pilgrims escaped from in Europe because they were persecuted when they formed their own beliefs somewhat different from what the state church had dictated. This forcing upon the masses one particular faith was troubling, but no less troubling is this present day forcing of secularist humanist belief system in American culture. For too long we have tolerated their influence and our country has become divided. No longer is there a respect for people's belief in God coming from government, especially the Judeo-Christian God. Sadly, many people have chosen the god of money (Christians included) a selfish and materialistic lifestyle which leads to idol worship and what the Bible calls idolatry. Probably the most dangerous sin one can commit because it replaces God with a false god.

Let us all return to a respect for each other with a better attitude if possible, but there are many who promote war and hate. As a Christian I have no mandate to hate another person, but I do have a mandate to hate evil acts. Whether we be Christian or not we all have values we adopt and cherish, and hopefully there are enough values we can agree on, especially helpful would be our love of family, and a responsible work ethic. The Christian community needs to be patient and compassionate to those and with those we disagree with, but the Bible warns us of too much compromise. There is certainly a fine line, and sometimes it is difficult to know where that line is, but I do know that God is patient and can change a person in a miraculous manner no matter how old a person may be. So, as a Christian I also have a mandate to pray for those who reject the Christian God. Yes, I can live peacefully with an atheist or a secular humanist in all their variety, but it doesn't mean I have to agree with them, especially when they attempt to silence people of faith, and create laws to prevent public service, or create a new morality code of sort that is contrary to the Creator's laws. What laws are those you may ask; they are the Ten Commandments and the two great commandments Jesus gave "to love God with all your heart, mind, and soul," and "to love one's neighbor as much as you love yourself." Of course, none of us are perfect and many of us fall short of keeping God's commandments perfectly, but God has offered a provision. We all can be justified with God by our faith in believing and accepting his perfect Son, Jesus Christ, who committed no sin. If we believe in his sacrifice and agree with him that our sins need to be forgiven, and we are humble and contrite God will certainly forgive and offer his grace and mercy. This is God's heart, and he wants all men to repent and trust in him. I know this is true because I challenged God to prove his love and existence to me when I was in Viet Nam, serving in the Air Force. It was a quite night, looking into an unbelievable sky full of stars; I just shouted out to God, "If you are real then prove yourself to me!" Well, he didn't just appear at that moment, but what he did do was to bring a person of strong faith into my life the very next day, and helped me immensely in solidifying my faith and walk with Christ. Christ became very personal to me at that moment when I believed and asked his forgiveness, and that faith remains with me today. There is a verse in the Bible that says "if you seek me, you will find me."

It is wrong that our society and government prevents a fair debate on the truest intentions of the Constitution, and the overwhelming evidence that our founding fathers were strengthened and given extraordinary wisdom by their reliance and trust in their Judeo-Christian God. Today, however it is a different story and people of faith are often slandered, and misrepresented and treated with malicious contempt, especially if they should attempt to do public service.

Have you ever wondered why America became a great nation? Some would say we are a melting pot of great people, or that our great wisdom and intelligence, and our perseverance to be free. Some might say because of great leaders or the form of government and democratic values. All of this is partially true, but in my way of thinking there is someone greater than the human spirit. Certainly, there is strong evidence that our beginnings in America were a unified few who aspired to have religious Christian freedoms, and this led to other god-like freedoms. Freedoms of speech, free worship, rights to own property and to provide for one's own protection, and a great vision that a government would be led by God, and a government that gave opportunity and a fair voice to its people.

The humble people who came to America were no more that a band of mostly poor folks who took a bold step of faith to venture into a new land. People, who possessed very little in material wealth, were in fact rich in faith and relied on there Christian God to lead them and provide for them. Quite possibly I have an idealistic view on the Pilgrims, but I know they were human and failed in common ways like all of us do, but I chose to believe that our great God intervened on there behalf to help America become a beacon light to the world. With all the mistakes of an imperfect people we stumbled many time as evidenced by the Civil War, and selfish land grabbing's, and racial hatred. Still, with these failures our imperfect history is common with other nations. Truly, this is not an attempt to excuse America for what it has done wrong, but there is also strong evidence of things done right! What other nation sacrificed so many to free slaves? What other nation has sent so many missionaries into the world to help guide them to a genuine faith in God, or has fought world wars in foreign lands to protect their freedoms without stealing their land? What other nation has helped in humanitarian relief to the extent that America has done? America has also been a faithful friend and supporter to tiny Israel since its becoming a nation in 1948. Our creator God has not forgotten these deeds, and he has rewarded America with protections and blessings, and as Americans we still have a great freedom of speech to propagate his truth. But, ask yourself, will God's protection and blessing continue if we allow godless and unjust laws to rule our land that exclude biblical truth from the public forum? Lets be clear, the socialist and humanistic mindset in America today whether knowingly or not is leading us towards a destructive path. Our Constitution does not advocate socialistic laws or government to steal from its people. The notion or ideology that says it is okay to trample on the God-given rights of a free people so long as it benefit's the state is totally foreign to the American republic and democracy. Many in our society have a maniacal fear about religious fanaticism where they (leftist politicians, liberal media) commonly misrepresent and compare Christians to the Taliban or some other unfair comparison of religious fanaticism. Nothing could be further from the truth. True faith and service coming from churches have blessed this country more than anyone will ever know or appreciate.

It is true that religious fanaticism is dangerous as we all can clearly see in some Arabic societies, and even some religious sects in American society. The Bible is clear in 1 John 4:20, "If anyone says, "I love God," yet hates his neighbor, he is a liar." This truth applies to all theocracy faiths of Judaism, Islam, and Christianity. We should never forget the history lessons of godless regimes who were led by fanatical religious governments, but no less dangerous is a fanatical secular ideology. Should we forget the atrocities of Communist nations of Russia, China, Cuba, South America, and others who led many to their deaths because they dared to resist. Can we learn from Nazi Germany, a national socialist country who became complicit with a murderous dictator? The "isms" of communism, fascism, totalitarianism, socialism, humanism, secularism, all lead to stolen birthrights of a free people. America is getting dangerously close to devaluating the priceless worth of a human being, and the godless push whether it is seen in euthanasia, abortion, or harmful alternative lifestyles that are being pushed on us as something that is normal. Gay lifestyles are morally wrong and God has spoken against it. Have you read about Sodom and Gomorrah? As Christians we should show compassion and have understanding towards those trapped in these immoral lifestyles, but again we should not be tolerant in our acceptance that the gay lifestyle is something that some people are born with, or something as normal. People, for whatever reason choose this kind of life, and they are in rebellion against God. Immoral decadence misleads our children away from God's definition of marriage and away from God's family design. Immoral practices should not be encouraged or be tolerated with passive attitudes. History can teach us that tolerating such lifestyles has led to the destruction of many societies. The Roman Empire is one example that we can learn from, if we choose to. In America we have too many politicians that lack the moral wisdom to see the harm of re-defining marriage.

All of our countries problems whether they be illegal immigration, drug wars, Iraqi and Afghanistan wars, greedy companies, national debt, poor education, healthcare issues, or any other governmental concerns are all trumped as being important, but if God was asked what would he say? The strength of our country is the family structure that our creator designed. Who are those who dare re-define it? We all have a conscience of what is right and what is wrong, and whether you believe it or not our creator put it there for a reason. I believe God pleads with us to trust him to follow his great laws, and without forcing us he gently provides the evidence of creation, and human examples of his grace and power in changing for good the lives of many of us who do not deserve it!

CHAPTER 3

SECULAR VS. CHRISTIAN

*S*ecular by Webster definition means "not connected to a church," or not religious in the church context. Religion can mean belief in God or gods, and can mean a specific system of beliefs or code. Since religion has a dual meaning the neo-agnostics and atheists use this to their advantage claiming they are not a religion. I mention this because America has leaned more secular than Christian over the past fifty years, but in our countries previous history things were different. Secularists were a minority. Still, today 80% of Americans claim some association with Christianity, and 95% celebrate Christmas. Although, some lack a genuine faith of the Christian community the fact remains that the sentiments at the core beliefs are decidedly pro-Christian.

Much of the media, the left-wing political establishment, and rabidly anti-Christian minorities are sounding-off at every opportunity. Then we have elitist points of view coming from major networks aired to put into question the credibility of the foundational, biblical essence of the Christian faith. The blatant agenda driven goal is to malign Christians, and attempt to compare the faithful to terrorists, and that evangelicals have a unified, conspiratorial plan to elect an ultra-fundamental kind of government. Oh really! Actually, the very thing they are accusing

Christians of is the very thing they are espousing, and their vision to keep our government and schools exclusively secular.

As a civil use description we are called a secular government because we are not governed by any Church. This however, is not to imply Christians should have no influence or involvement is public office or schools. To say we are a secular democracy and use it to silence Christians and discriminate against them is wrong-headed and mis-leading. More accurately, we are a pluralistic government representing all people of varying belief systems with first amendment rights.

Belief Systems

Belief systems that are not labeled religion are the un-named churches of atheism and humanism, and many of them are supported by civil activist groups who are focused on attacking traditional Judeo-Christian beliefs and bent on a cultural war in America. They often cry foul when they are offended in some trivial way. They twist and turn the real truth, and use partial truths to justify their perverted thinking. Frankly they know little of our Constitutional freedoms and dishonor our founding fathers vision for America. The founder of the ACLU was a communist. I wonder how many people know that fact! This group especially is aggressive in attacking our freedoms of speech and freedoms of religion. What they really believe and promote is state control, and a total secular environment and limiting individual freedoms. These dangerous folks permeate our judicial system who attempt to re-write our Constitution, and make ridiculous rulings that are not centered on the truest intents of Constitutional writings. They often reward the guilty and punish the victim, and pretend to protect our civil rights, and attempt to intimidate those of us who know their game plan. The American Civil Liberties Union is a contrast in terms of who they really are, because they are not loyal to America because of their continual attempts to subvert our form of government.

Organizations like this have done nothing to contribute to the greatness of America, and they only divide us. Let us as patriots try to respect each other no matter what belief system you may lean towards. I for one believe in the "golden rule," that we should treat and respect others with the same degree as we respect ourselves. To me, this biblical formula has proven its worthiness since our nations beginning. Why should we abandon it now? But, then again, that doesn't mean that I should apologize for what I believe, nor does it mean that I shouldn't stand against those who try destroying Constitutional freedoms.

Consider

Religion defined by Webster can mean belief in God or gods, and can mean a specific system of beliefs or code. Since religion is not solely defined as only a belief in God, any belief system can honestly be called a religion. When considering voting for a candidate of any religious persuasion whether it be Hinduism, Buddasism, Hinduism, Baha'ism, Secularism, Atheism, Agnosticism, Mormonism, or any other "ism," please remember an American historical fact. Our founding fathers adopted the Judeo-Christian faith, and all gave great credence and respect to the Holy Scriptures.

Of all the belief systems listed above, only Mormonism clones the Christian faith, but there are distinct differences. The most serious deviation and doctrinal difference is their view on the deity of Jesus Christ. The Bible teaches that Christ is the "only begotten Son of God" and co-equal in the tri-unity of the God-head, but we never become co-equal with Jesus Christ. The Mormon faith teaches that after a life of good works one is transcended into heaven becoming a "son of God," co-equal with Jesus Christ.

Actually, all religions other than Christianity attack the deity of Christ and adopt a system of good works that is promoted over the good work that Christ accomplished when he died on the cross and shed his blood for the sin of every person in this world. Through faith in Christ we are reconciled into a right relationship with God. Galatians 2:21 states; "do not set aside the grace of God, for if righteousness could be gained through the law, Christ died for nothing."

Please understand that our forefathers never envisioned any religion other than the Judeo-Christian faith, and when they said their should be no "religious test" to run for office they meant to hold back scrutiny against the varying Christian denominations of that time.

Mike Huckabee is influenced less by the power of money, and is not ashamed to stand on Christian principles, someone our forefathers would recognize and support. It is sad that America has to some degree lost its first love for God, but Mike is a breath of fresh air, and offers hope to America. Although he is not a presidential candidate this time around, he does have a successful television show on Fox, and I think this kind of exposure will help him in the future if he so chooses to serve our country in some capacity.

Paganism vs. Christianity

There is nothing revolutionary in the notion that atheism is temporarily winning the day, nor is novel that Christianity is being pronounced dead, and its followers are persecuted. In fact, evidence shows that Christianity actually increases when persecution occurs. Ever since the earliest beginnings of Christianity in Corinth, Ephesus, and many Mediterranean coastline civilizations where the apostles Peter and Paul and the gang promoted the great movement; their leaders and followers have always suffered unjust hardships and judgments. Peter chose crucifixion up-side down because he said he was not worthy to be crucified as Christ was, and Paul was also jailed and beaten many times before he was martyred. In fact, all the faithful apostles were murdered, except for John who went to the Isle of Patmos where he had visions of the future and wrote the book "Revelations." For Christianity to advance it almost seems that it must endure hardships. This truth bears out as one looks back to Rome. The citizens of Rome were "statists" and they were pagans and knew nothing of Christianity. Nero was by far the most wicked ruler who wanted to destroy the Christian movement, who promoted the murdering of thousands of Christians by feeding them to lions in the Roman arena of entertainment. It wasn't until after this massive persecution, and conversions in the Caesar household that things began to change in Rome. Eventually, Rome was declared a Christian nation by Constantine.

You see, the human desire to return to paganism is not something new, and Christianity has a long history when God has intervened and helped human depravity back to its senses, but their will be a day when his longsuffering and patience will end, and he will allow the human race choose its destruction through paganism. What is paganism? You could say paganism is license to do what ever you want, ignoring the ten commandments of God, and choosing a false morality code of their choosing or a code enforced by the state. What does paganism lead too? Paul explained human depravity in the first chapter of Romans. It would be a world of ungodly judges" who distort God's truth, who worship man more than God." Sexual decadence would rule the day and eventually God would give them up to a reprobate mind, "filled with unrighteous acts of fornication, covetousness, maliciousness, envy, murder, debate, deceit, malignity, whisperers, backsliders, proud, boastful, inventers of evil things, disobedient to parents, without understanding, covenant breakers, without natural affection, implacable, unmerciful." Well, this is the kind of "hell on earth" reality that any society will face if it chooses "paganism" over "Christianity!" I hope God will not give up on America, but if good people choose to do little in protecting their children from the cultural and liberal invasion that is leading them headlong into paganism. How would God view such apathy?

Looking back at American history was it paganism (many gods) that helped shape America, or was it monotheism (one god) belief system? The truth be told, it was Christian love and biblical truth that broke the bondage of addictions and pagan beliefs, and it is still true today. God help us who share this great faith to start a revival in America.

Referring back to Mr. Obama's speech in Ankara, Turkey he said America is no longer a Christian nation but "a nation of citizens who are bound by ideals and set of values." Question needs to be asked, whose values is he espousing? Obviously he is repulsing Judeo-Christian fundamentals of governance, but what rules will apply? By what standard will they be administered? Who will be the judge? It will be the rulers of the statist religion, and not God, even though they will claim that God is with them in their ungodly decisions.

Polls have been taken that indicate 62% of Americans believe that America is a Christian nation. Our Christian heritage is our firm foundation of hope and stability that has kept us free for over 200 years. Yet that stability can be destroyed in less than a year if we choose massive social bills like "national health care," "cap and trade (environmental tax), or "global warming iniatives" that will lead us into massive debt and will spur the end of capitalism and entrepreneurship. The future holds a lot of uncertainty and little hope especially if we allow misguided leaders to continue leading us. As a Christian we have a mandate to pray for our leaders, but if they do not change towards truly representing the people, then we need to pray and support the right leaders to replace them.

As Americans we need to ask ourselves this question; do we envision a pagan country as I described earlier, or do we envision a nation of people who love their country, love freedom and fight for freedom of oppressed people, love decency and honesty, pay their taxes, and promote free giving to help communities and needy people. Remembering also, that this kind of love must come from free will, and not mandated by some governmental program. This kind of mandate is not Christianity, but statism. We must respect the right of those who choose to worship differently as long as that faith is peaceful, and we must respect the right of those who choose not to worship at all. Yes, we can peacefully co-exist with an atheist, but let us be clear that Christians should not be passive if an atheist movement tries to destroy our freedoms that God has inherently given to all people of faith. Quite the contrary, we should rise up and protect our freedoms. God will never reward passivism or apathy. Christians and all people of good will must throw off all unjust laws of political correctness, and go back to the tried and true guide book that led us to greatness; the Bible. This kind of faith that relied on the Holy Scriptures is the kind of faith that our forefathers trusted in and helped leads us to American exceptionalism. Foreign nations were astonished at the rate of growth and prosperity of America in the eighteenth century, so much so that a famous Frenchman, Alexis Tocqueville, was sent to America to investigate why this young country prospered, and his conclusions were simply put," that American's were people of faith, religion, and Christianity."

Israel

It has been said, and I believe it to be true, that "those who ignore the mistakes of the past are doomed to repeat it." The United States and Great Britain have proven at least in part to be Israel's best allies and supporters of democracy in the Middle East. General Balflour of the British army helped establish Jewish immigrants to re-establish themselves into their homeland in the early 1900's. It was called the "Balflour Declaration." This man of faith had a vision to help God's people back to the promise land. But, the British soon abandoned their loyalty to Israel years later. It appears that the United States is following a similar path of abandonment. Today, much of our support is tacit at best, but still we do remain a supporter in some sense by providing a sale of arms and trade, but in other areas of diplomacy we are not a true friend. U.S. diplomatic policies are increasingly pushing Israel towards more concessions to the Palestinians who are controlled by Hama's, who are intent upon Israel's destruction. Hama's is an Islamic Republic who is directly funded by Iran. The U.S. knows that Iran is behind all the terrorism against Israel and our country, but why are we timid in stopping Iran? Why are we ignoring the fact that Iran is directly supplying the Taliban, and more importantly why are we abandoning our support for Israel, and telling them not to attack

Iran's nuclear build-up? Why is the U.S. ignoring the fact that Russia is supplying Iran with nuclear materials? Peaceful Arab states are beside themselves with anxiety about Iran's nuclear capability. Why was Obama's administration complacent about Iran's nuclear build-up, when clearly there is no hope of negotiations with a radical Iranian state? Pro-Israel female commentator Melanie Phillips has said that Prime Minister Benjamin Netanyahu "must take the message to the ordinary American people that America is now run by a man who is intent on sacrificing Israel for a reckless and amoral political strategy which will put America and the rest of the free world at risk."

I firmly believe that our countries protection and blessing comes from our support of Israel. This has much to do with God's promise to bring back his people and nation to its homeland. Should we now forget that Israel is at the root of our Judeo-Christian heritage? Do we ignore the importance that Israel is the only true democracy in the middle-east? Is it only happanstance that Israel poses one of the most powerful militaries in the world? Little Israel, one of the smallest nations on earth with few nations who support them, how do they continue to survive? To me, it would be foolish not to think that God is there true protector. There occupied land is a small fraction of what the Arabic nations occupy, and why are they so incensed about destroying the tiny nation? In my humble opinion, the mere fact that Israel does exist is testimony to the fact that God exists. And, if you believe in God then one must believe in God's arch enemy whom I believe is at the root of the entire disturbance surrounding Israel. Actually, Israel's promise land goes much larger than what they own at present. There boundaries should extend further north into Jordan and Syria, further east bordering the Euphrates River in Iraq, and further south as well. But they don't occupy the land, because they are trying to be at peace with the world. All their concessions and efforts will not bring them peace, until they look to the one that can truly give them peace. As people of Abrahamic faith, we need to pray for Israel and its leaders.

How do our U.S. diplomats have the gall to push Israel to give up more of its lands and Jerusalem? Who are we to tell Israel what to do, especially on matters of their sovereignty and the stealing of their land?

How would we like it if a bigger, more powerful nation came to us and said you must give up some of your land for the sake of fabricated peace treaties that mean absolutely nothing?

Only a few Arabic states are at peace with Israel, currently Egypt is one country that does recognize its right to exist, but only after Israel defeated the Egyptian invasion in the Yom Kipper war. Maybe Egypt has recognized in some sense that they were defeated by a far inferior military fighting force and have come to realize that the only way Israel could have won was through God's intervention. I really do not know if this is true, but the Egyptians have learned that it is better to respect Israel and has helped bring peace between the two countries. But, the leadership in Egypt is changing towards a more radical element in the Muslim Brotherhood, and attitudes towards Israel survival is quickly changing. Many Arabic nations have radical elements and groups especially among the Shiite's. Syria and Iran are mostly assuredly behind the turmoil in the middle-east and forging new alliances among various groups. These groups are unified upon the Islamic Hadith teachings that carry nearly the same weight as the Koran. Its writings are hateful towards the Jews, and they believe that Palestine is Islamic land, and that there is no solution to the problem except through jihad. In 1988, Hama's and the PLO the charter writings that basically calls on all Palestinians to become shahids, or martyrs, for the cause of destroying Israel and establishing an Arab state based on the Qur'an's civil and religious laws. In short, it is all about domination and no tolerance towards infidels. These groups are Hama's, Lebanese Hezbollah, Syria, and Osama Bin Laden's al-Qaeda and some Sunni-Muslim groups are aligning with and supported by Shiite Iran.

Iran's leader Mahmoud Ahmadinejad has repeatedly said they will never recognize Israel's right to exist as a nation, and has threatened annilation quoting that they will "drive them into the sea." Rewinding to ancient history wasn't there a similar threat from an Egyptian Pharaoh who attempted to drive the Israelites into the sea, but if the Bible is accurate it was the Egyptian army that perished in the sea. We should never forget what history can teach us, and we should not take lightly God's promise to Israel; "The Lord appeared to us in the past, saying:

"I have loved you with an everlasting love; I have drawn you with loving-kindness, I will build you up again and you will be rebuilt, O Virgin Israel" (Jer. 31). Another biblical promise is that nations who bless Israel will be blessed, and those nations who curse Israel will be cursed. In Genesis 12:3 "I will bless those who bless you. And I will curse Him who curses you: And in you all the families of the earth shall be blessed."

In helping to understand the hatred promoted through Islam we need to be aware of the Khartoum Resolution of 1967 when leaders of eight Arab countries agreed on policy base on three declarations: No peace with Israel. No recognition of Israel. No negotiations with Israel. Moshe Sharon, retired professor of early Islamic history spoke on counter terrorism in Israel and on the nature of Islam. He said, "It is a mistake to differentiate between radical and peaceful Islam." He thinks the western policies fail to understand Islamic resolve and belief system of looking forward to a messianic "Mahdi." The Shiite messiah, the Twelfth Imam or Mahdi. They believe he will come to rule the world and all other religions, and he will appear during an apocalypse. Another words, a world war is necessary. This is why we should stop Iran from obtaining nuclear weapons before the radical in Iran lead the world into "Armageddon." Moshe has also said concerning the Arab-Israeli conflict "the root of the problem between us (Israelis) and the Arab world is Islam. Islam is not only a religion, it is culture, politics…a state; Islam is everything. Moshe dismisses that treaties as only "pieces of paper," and have no meaning whatsoever. It is difficult to deny what Moshe has said, because past history proves that his words are true. The sooner our nation's leaders understand this the safer the world will be; but do not look at the Obama administration to defend Israel. In Obama's own words he has said, "We do not consider ourselves a Christian nation." Shortly thereafter, he proclaimed America as "one of the largest Muslim countries," when he said 1200 mosques exist in our nation. Another slap to Christianity and to America's faith based community, when the white house announced it would not observe the National Day of Prayer. It gives me no pleasure to say it, but Mr. Obama is calling for a curse on America when he has no resolve to protect Israel, and no reliance on the Judeo-Christian God to protect America. President Obama says he is a supporter of Israel, yet he strives to divide Jerusalem by 2012, and uses the Iran crisis to achieve his goal. His intention to undermine Israel by supporting Palestinian claims to establish statehood when he goes along with the UN and Arab League. The deception here is his saying he supports Israel, when clearly he is doing all he can to undermine Israel's survival. Obama gives no evidence that he believes in the warning or blessing to nations that take heed to God's promise in Genesis 12:1-3. I'll leave it up to you to read it.

There are no boundaries to which Israel's adversaries will go to disenfranchise the Jewish people who reside in the Holy Land. The NY Times ambushed an Israeli diplomat, when a reporter (Friedman) had accused Israel of being a "spoiled child, crazy, and extremist." But the real extremists are the radical Muslim factions who wage war against Israel continually, who still launch attacks with rockets and bombs, and the NY Times still doesn't report it! Herein lays the outrage. The Palestinians and Arab League make ludicrous claims that the Jews have no historical evidence that the Jewish people's homeland is in Jerusalem and the Holy Land. The fact is that Muslims are waging war and are relentless in their efforts to purge the Middle East of all Christians. Little is being reported that "some two million" (Israel My Glory; An Onslaught Exodus-pg. 12), fleeing Christians have had to leave the Middle East. This exodus is clearly seen from the Christians in Egypt, Sudan, Iraq, Iran, and many other Arab nations. Yet our president has a blind eye to the plight of suffering Christians, and rather chooses to support radical Muslim groups instead of supporting Christians. How can a president who says he is a Christian be so blind and cruel to ignore supporting Israel and suffering Christians who are trying to survive in the Middle East? The answer to that question in my opinion is that he is not blind, but calculated, and knows exactly what he is doing; and what he is doing is against God.

On May 24. 2011 Israeli Prime Minister, Benjamin Netanyahu addressed the US Congress when he said, "Israel has no better friend than America, and America has no better friend than Israel. We stand together to defend Israel. We stand together to defend democracy. We

stand together to advance peace. We stand together to fight terrorism...
In an unstable Middle East, Israel is the one anchor of stability. In
a region of shifting alliances, Israel is America's unwavering ally.
Israel has always been pro-American. My friends, you don't need to
do nation building in Israel. We're already built. You don't need to
export democracy to Israel. We've already go it. You don't need to send
American troops to defend Israel. We defend ourselves. You've been
very generous in giving us tools to do the job of defending Israel on
our own. Thank you all."

As you consider these words from an ally of the United States, why
would our government ever consider be-friending Israel?

CHAPTER 4

ANTI-AMERICAN

We as American's really need to be aware that we have many forces that are hard at work at promoting disharmony and disunity, and what they want is a different kind of America. Not what our founding forefathers envisioned, but a powerful state controlled kind of government, and they want to fleece our wealth in promoting a socialist utopia. It is my opinion that they are increasingly organized and coordinated in their attacks upon our individual freedoms. This list is not exhaustive, but I will mention a few that are well known by most people; {the UN, Arab League, Liberal media outlets, current White House Administration, NAACP, Democratic Party leadership, liberal politicians from both parties, liberal professors at universities, liberal and activist judges, ACLU, and George Soros}.

Currently we hear a constant drumbeat of blaming the Republicans, or our previous president George Bush, or just anybody is to blame that doesn't believe or support the Obama Administration. Anybody who disagrees with Obama's policies is automatically deemed racist or un-American. This is the old Democratic game plan of blaming conservatives in general, or anyone who has wealth is judged as guilty, except those wealthy folks who happen to be Democrat. It is humorous to me that they continue to demonize the rich conservatives as the main culprit to the economic crisis. Oil companies are always the problem, so they say. An interesting fact is that 90% of oil companies worldwide are actually owned by governments and not private enterprises. In America the percentage are a bit higher for private oil companies, but it should not be overlooked that America receives 70% of oil reserves from foreign nations. Yet so much is made of our oil companies profit margins, and blaming them for the high gas prices. The Democrats always smear the oil companies who are private enterprises as greedy and un-American because they make a profit. But don't all private business companies seek a profit? Without profit how could they hire employees? All clear headed thinking Americans know that all the Obama administration is trying to do is to deflect blame on the private oil companies, when clearly the blame rest squarely on the governments out of control spending. Also, the government is refusing to allow oil drilling in our own country, eliminating jobs for Americans, as well causing an even greater dependence on foreign oil. This foreign dependence also rests on the fact that the government refused to build new refineries, which actually causes us to ship our own oil to foreigners which only adds to the cost of oil. The government is always pushing for higher taxes, and more tax policies, their relentless support for ridiculous EPA regulations. So foolish and unnecessary are their ways, and all their refusals and unjust tax schemes are at the heart of the problems of energy costs and high gas prices at the pump. Ask yourself; are you better off financially since Obama has been President? What were the prices at the pump before Obama came to office? The average per gallon of gas was about one dollar and eighty cents. Now were paying about three fifty a gallon, and in some regions over four dollars a gallon. History has a way of repeating itself, because during President Carters era gas prices also plummeted. The blame is squarely on the Democrats for high gas prices, and their unprincipled attacks on oil companies should not be forgotten by voting Americans.

The "Robin Hood" politics of stealing from the rich in order to give to the government still reigns popular to some Americans who are fooled into this kind of ideological thinking that it is somehow a fair and just way to do things. Will you stay with me as I try to break this down? First of all, is their anything moral or fair in stealing? The eighth commandment to Moses was "Thou Shalt Not Steal!" The commandment is plain and simple to understand. Are there exceptions to the rule? Can we alter God's commandment by conjuring up the idea that it is for a good purpose and better government? Or can we say that we only take from those who don't need it? Even if one does not have a religious reason of morality, our own laws prosecute against stealing. This whole idea of taking money from the rich makes the broad assumption that all wealthy people gained their wealth through stealing or corruptible means. This idea of painting a broad brush against all wealthy persons is an unjust and immoral law. It is true that some wealth has been gained by deception or corruptible means, but many have earned their wealth through hard work, planning, and taking risk, and it should not be overlook that wealthy persons provide jobs for many people. The broad deception imposed by our government today is that they will provide for the needy, but government does not produce money. It only takes money from anyone who has it! Ask yourself, does the government really provide a healthy environment between the rich and the poor? The answer is an emphatic no. Have you taken a close look at those who rely on government hand-outs? These people are unmotivated to do anything productive in their lives, and the only thing they look forward to be their unearned check. Any people who think that something is owed to them as entitlements are only hurting themselves and it leads to social un-rest, and instead of uniting people it causes division and anger. This kind of class warfare is what caused the Communist revolution in Russia and China, and the French Revolution and the murdering of millions. Government dependence only reduces people to be slaves of the government, and ends up stealing their God given right to dignity and freedom.

President Obama says many lofty things, but his promises ring empty, and little if anything productive is being done. He has not been honest with the American people. He claims taxes will not go up "one dime" on people who make less than 250, 000. This bold claim is blatantly false. The Bush tax cuts have been undermined, and back door taxes are hitting small business owners and the working class with tax increases. Taxes come from many directions, on product, EPA regulations, state and locale, and on income. For people of modest income are being hit on increases taxes on gasoline, real estate tax, state and local fees, and the list goes on and on. The Cap and Trade bill which was almost passed would have increased an average family an additional 25 thousand dollars a year of which Obama and the Democrats wanted to pass. President Obama continues to spend trillion of dollars on Obama care, bailouts, and stimulus money that has stimulated nothing. Remember, not one job is lost in the private sector by cutting taxes. But if taxes were to be cut to private business, then they could hire employees on a large scale. All responsible Americans know how to budget their money. They prioritize what they must pay for first, and paying off their debts is crucial to financial freedom. Our government has yet to learn this invaluable lesson.

Indifference: A Friend to Socialism

The best way to defeat the domestic enemy within our nation (advocates for a new and dangerous kind of government), is to become engaged and involved with people who know and respect our Constitution. We have all heard the common responses and clichés from people not engaged in politics. They say things like, "it doesn't matter who you vote for, nothing will change," or "don't talk to me about politics or religion." Either they are not knowledgeable on the issue, or they feel there is no hope or future, no apologetic, no discussion, just a complacent attitude. If attitudes do not change for the better and people do not vote to remove bad politicians and replace them with good people who honor the Constitution, then we will get more of the same. Way too many Americans are naïve to what is going on, and that is what clever politicians are relying on. Some people are centered on narcissistic living, or they may be responsible folks that are just concerned on their own personal lives with family and making a living. This is quite normal and necessary, but ignoring politics and how it affects our form of government is a very serious problem in America. To preserve our great nation we must get involved in something we believe in, and with vision and passion we can alter and stop the indifference. The reason why there are so many arguments about politics, belief systems, and religion is because they are so vital to real meaning and purpose in life. They are related like "brothers" and the battle of ideas are worth the battle if we want to be a free people.

Today, so many people are questioning the "Tea Party Movement." Accusing them of this, that, and the other, and most all of the attacks are untrue. They are a groundswell of concerned and patriotic people, diverse as well in race and in party affiliation. Recent estimates say the movement consists of forty-percent democrat and independent voters. They believe the Constitution should be upheld, the basic law of the land, and should not be altered by liberal activist judges and liberal politicians who simply do so because they have been allowed to do so. If more people understood what the Constitution said, then obviously they would not stand by and do nothing. That is why the "Tea Party" is so important and so threatening to the liberal masses, because they know the movement is credible and a peaceful movement, and they are worried about losing their power. Liberals are frantically uniting to discredit the movement with venom and slanderous accusations. We who believe in the American dream and Constitution, and who cherish freedoms must unite to discredit their false claims. Truth is not an easy thing to defend; often it is the most difficult. People are quick to judge before they know the facts, especially when they are not open to alternative media that are not anchored to the "left." The liberal media and all of their cohorts are so desperate they are promoting radical ideologues' pretending to be "tea party" members. Why do they do this? Simply put, they want to fool enough people into thinking the "tea party" members are radical and violent. Tea party members are normal family oriented folks who believe and practice a respectable lifestyle within their communities and are people of faith, or people who want to believe, and people who love America.

Why did our founding fathers believe in God? Why did they write in their documents so much about their faith in Christ? Even with so many diverse denominations they came together to oppose the tyranny of King George. Why did America grow so quickly and powerfully? A famous Frenchman, Alexis Tocqueville, was sent to America to investigate the phenomenon, and this is what he said, "that American's were people of faith, religion, and Christianity."

Early Americans were an amazing people with great energy and faith in God, and fought wars to give us all a new birth of freedom. The Declaration of Independence begins with, "These truths are self-evident that all men are created equal, and endowed with certain inalienable rights of life, liberty, and the pursuit of happiness." Martin Luther King Jr. spoke these great words to his people; a great man of faith admonished many to stand up to racism, but to always stand for peace. He was the reason they marched in controlled crowds, and although they were beaten at times, they remained peaceful. This great example of a peaceful march for truth is what the "Tea Party" is all about. May they continue to rally for better government, and may they continue to unite in peace, and may the truth that they stand for be a beacon light to those who lack knowledge and insight into our great Constitution.

Socialism Is Not Compassionate

President Obama has made comments saying that he is a Christian, and that we should all take care of our brothers. I do not question his personal belief in God, but I do question his convictions in his promotion that government is responsible to be our "brother's keeper." I do not see evidence in the Bible that promotes this idea. Jesus did not hold political views, nor did he promote any preferred kind of government to enhance his mission. Jesus did give us the "Sermon on the Mount," and demonstrated numerous examples of compassion. He instructed his disciples in love, and he did not promote a hateful rebellion against the Romans, even though the Romans were hateful towards his people. A much as possible, he promoted peace and non-violence towards the Roman government. In Luke 7:3 Jesus recognized a Roman centurion who had a remarkable faith and believed that Jesus could heal his servant by just speaking the word. Jesus said, "I have not found such great faith even in Israel." He truly loved even his enemies. Jesus did challenge the religious leaders about their laws that did not honor God, and he did promote his relationship with God the Father, their oneness, and he said "I came to do my father's will" which was to die on a cross for the sins of the people, to make way for all to be redeemed and made acceptable to God. This great sacrifice of love was not only for Israel, but for all people who have faith. But the religious leaders of that time rejected him, even after he had done great miracles. You see, they were jealous of him, and they couldn't understand how he could do such miracles without giving them honor, and his ignoring their man-made laws. It is no different today, we have governmental leaders who want to be god-like, live like kings, and every once in a while throw crumbs to the crowd. But what they are actually doing is creating class-warfare and stealing money, and stealing honor that belongs to God. A Christian's mandate to do service that honors God is a personal responsibility, and a choice we must all make. It should never be force upon us by some kind of social justice of higher taxes, or "Robin Hood" politics of taking from the rich and giving to the poor. The murderous revolution of Marxism and Communism got its rise from corrupt officials promoting class warfare. The same thing can be said in the French Revolution, where nobles and men of wealth were ostracized, scorned an executed, and lands were taken. This kind of tyranny never honors God. Only God can change a heart to do what is right, and to do it for the right reasons. America has always been a giving people, and a giving nation, much of which derives from Judeo-Christian values. Let us go back to the time tested formula for meeting the needs of the poor. Not a forced governmental social program, that only leads to a bigger and more powerful government.

Leaders of socialism and progressive movements in our country are really not compassionate. Even some churches have fallen prey to the delusion and persuasion of social justice. These believers fail to recognize that their lack of faith and obedience to live in peace, and falling prey to coveting a neighbor's wealth is at the root of their susceptibility to social ideology. Marxist and Communist leaders are actually atheist and agnostic and replace God with images of themselves. This kind of false worship is pure idolatry. Worshipping a false idol (or person) instead of worshipping and honoring our creator. If socialism is compassionate why has it brutally murdered people for the sake of their ideology? Was not Nazi Germany a country ruled by a government of National Socialism? Please, reconsider supporting any candidate or incumbent who is advocating and advancing socialism and progressive movements in our country.

Who Are The Real Advocates of Hate?

What is considered a hate crime by our federal government is increasingly targeting any free speech that they do not agree with, or does not measure up to their political correctness. What they are actually doing is legislating their brand of morality. A famous founding father, Thomas Jefferson once said, "Almighty God has created the mind free…all attempts to influence it by temporal punishments or burdens…are a departure from the plan of the Holy Author of our religion." To me, the real crime is that our elected officials no longer follow this plan, but devise devious plans to thwart our founding fathers wisdom. In doing so they also oppose the truest intents of the law of the land, the Constitution, and Declaration of Independence. Who is really committing the crime? To me, it is directly coming from elected officials, activist judges and liberal media, but indirectly coming from those who vote them into office.

Increasingly, conservative radio hosts, tea party members, Christians, and basically all people who honor our Constitution are the convenient target of alleged hate crimes. Lobbying pressure from homosexual activists and pro-Muslim groups are actively promoting ideas of sensitivity when they are offended by Christian broadcasters whether on radio or television. This kind of complaint will in my opinion be the basis of legislature that will be labeled a hate crime, and the breaking of this law will require no violence at all. Legislation exists that uses the term "bodily injury" that includes things like, "mental trauma." So even if Christians broadcasters make every effort not to offend, it will really not matter if they have good intentions or not. Eventually, the freedom for Christians to spread the "good news" will become a thing of the past, because their kind of speech will be labeled a "hate crime." The same will happen to conservative or independent radio hosts who question the government's decision making. These brave speakers attempting to defend and protect our American freedoms are already being labeled "propagators of hate." Former American president, Bill Clinton has recently spoken a war of words against what he deems as radical "tea partiers," and radical conservative radio persons. What he said, were "these propagators of hate deserve to be silenced."

The right to free speech is eroding at a quick pace, and unless the American people stop the onslaught on our God given rights by standing up to socialist/Marxist bullies in government, America will not be the "land of the free." It is high time to bully them out of office. The false morality code of our government's political correctness should not be allowed to become so powerful it removes Judeo-Christian morality and free speech. If that ever happens, real sedition and tyranny has entered our land, and a cruel dictator is on the horizon.

Ideally, this world could be a better place if people would be less motivated by power and selfishness, but only God can change a heart. Obviously, the Obama administration has done a masterful job at demonizing the greed problem and focusing their attacks upon (insurance, auto, banks, CEO', wall street) in an all effort to promote class envy. Just another spoke in the wheel in promoting a government of socialism/Marxism. What the government is doing is taking the sin nature of man, that greedy and selfish part of us and using it to promote government control. Sure, there are some that are extremely greedy, scam artists and the like, but what the government is doing in taking over and dictating to states, banks, companies, citizens, and now Wall Street, is the biggest scam and takeover in American history. Let us not forget what Nazi Germany did in their establishment of "national socialism" in taking over companies and banks and peoples freedom, that led to the documented horror and atrocities that made them susceptible to a great orator and madman and atheistic regime.

Let us never allow a man leader or big government to become our god. This ideology comes directly from the gates of hell!

What Are Rights

Rights of the people are not unalterable when they re-write the rules. When groups and individuals are advocating anarchy and violence, this goes beyond the right of free speech. Minister Farrakhan routinely speaks in anger about his hate for America and stirring hatred among the people who listen to him. He has been a supporter of President Obama, but when the president supported the killing of Kaddafi, he actually called the President an assassin. Jessie Jackson who claims to be a voice for black Americans is always clamoring for reparations, which means more social programs and tax money we all would have to support. Is this a justified right to claim when the sins of slavery were paid for in full by Americans who sacrificed their lives in order to secure the rights of a free people. Phil Ayers who participated in an act of bomb terrorism, and is still promoting hatred and social revolution today. Would any decent thinking person believe that this radical person deserves the right to propagate his hate message to anybody? President Obama claims that he was" just a man in the neighborhood," but some think he is not divulging the full story on his relations with this man. Reverend Wright, an advocate of Black Liberation Theology, a belief system that I believe to be a perversion of true Christianity, continually preaches hate against America, and conspiratorial theories rousing up people to believe the way he does. How can it be that Mr.

Obama attended this church for twenty years and not be affected by his hate speech? How can it be that the liberal press reported nothing on this while Obama was promoting his candidacy? Didn't the American people deserve the right of an honest reporting on the matter? Don't the American people deserve to hear the truth about Mr. Obama's past associations? Of course they do, but the liberal press has not and will not report the truth when is harmful to their agenda, or when it hurts the candidate they choose to support. Do the media have the right to speak or write in half-truths? Does the media have the right to make up their own opinions, and distort the truth to advance anything they deem to be worthy? Isn't their real job supposed to be to just report the news in honesty and integrity? But news today is anything but that, and does the American people a disservice. A recent example of the liberal press doing a disservice to America is when they bore false witness against Herman Cain, promoting women to cast aspersions and false accusations against him, eventually causing him to withdraw. This tactic of bearing false witness against conservative people without evidence is a travesty that far too many people seem to condone. It is nothing more than filthy gossip and slander. Today we have a choice to listen to the media outlets that we believe do a better job of reporting the truth. But arriving at truth is always illusive and we really need to be careful that we don't believe everything we read or hear just because we find it interesting. We need to investigate and verify; this is our right and responsibility.

The youthful riots and protests at Wall Street and at banks, and even attempts at subways to stop people from going to work are going far beyond their right to assemble. When they occupy private and public property by putting up tents or living quarters, causing hygiene problems, security problems of life and property, is not a legal right. Because some mayors have been complicit with the protesters they have become embolden to act out. This is turn has led to criminal behavior of murder, rapes, theft, and excessive non-compliance with police.

Do we benefit from the accurate reporting of these events from all the media outlets? The answer to that question is an emphatic no we do not, and the reason for this is because the movement is supported by the Obama administration and the liberal media. Why would they support such actions of violent protest? I don't think they hoped for the violence to get out of hand, but they do support the idea of the ninety-nine percent who don't get their fair share, and pitting the have-nots against the extreme rich. This movement goes quite nicely with the ideology of socialism of which the Obama administration is wholeheartedly behind. Also, they needed a movement to counteract the powerful influence of the Tea Party. But because of the excessive behaviors of violence some think this will harm President Obama for his re-election goal. In any case, it is my firm belief that all people who advocate hate speech and motivate youthful minds with a kind of brainwashing that come from Marxist revolutionary people need to be put in jail. Any form of hate whether it is by words or actions are equally dangerous to a peaceful society. Lest I forget, a complicit media that fails to report or distort the truth by false reporting are to a great degree criminal in their behavior. President Obama constantly casts blame at the Republicans or any conservative who think differently of the president's ideas, or any people who do not want a Socialist/Marxist kind of government, and of course he does not openly admit securing a socialist government is his goal, but he has certainly hinted at it by repeating words like "hope and change." The President is not uniting America, and he carefully chooses the people and groups that support him, and continually cast blame at anyone who disagrees. I don't think he is acting in a presidential manner when he said, "if Congress will not act on his policies, he will act without them." When he becomes so embolden to say he will act without the approval of Congress then he is acting outside the boundaries of our Constitution, and is on dangerous ground to be impeached. The disappointing fact is that there are not enough conservative Republicans who have the will to stand up to this president. Always seemingly concerned about how they are being perceived by the people, they need to do what is right and principled affirming a full conviction of following the Constitution. As well, there are not enough Americans paying attention to the fact that his actions are not Constitutional per his enacting (government healthcare, company and mortgage bailouts), and putting our nation in critical debt endangering the survival of our nation.

Indoctrination in America

Clearly the radical left movement is promoting efforts to indoctrinate our children in our schools and in our government. These tactics are not unlike what Nazi Germany did to its children who were a powerful force and essential in their government take over. Strong efforts to indoctrinate Nazi belief systems at a very young age caused a sleeping nation to fall victim to a radical charismatic leader. Our current administration is feverishly allowing radical groups to infiltrate our government. Groups like ACORN, the SEIU which are promoting Obama's healthcare system. Glen Beck (radio host) has warned us that there are possibly 300 new radical groups entering our government. This is serious cause for alarm. Obama is promoting a youth movement in Americorps. Glen said that it is curious that the leader of Americorp was fired for no apparent reason, and now our president has the person he wants to advance radical socialism under the guise of community organizers. Not unlike what Hitler did when he promoted the "brown shirts." Hitler promoted hate groups against the Jewish community, and some of these hate groups are still in existence today. Remnants of these Arabic groups are now called Hezbollah, just one of many who have always hated the Jews.

In America we have tolerated hate groups as well, and today our president is complicit. In the past it was the KKK, but now it has become Planned Parenthood, NCCAP, ACORN, ACLU and others and their angry attack against the unborn, the elderly, our Constitution, our Judeo-Christian heritage, business people, and the overall spirit of liberty. White rich people and Jewish Americans and Christians are especially targeted as what is wrong with America. Hatred of a race of people flies in the face of morality and good will toward your neighbor, and is radically opposed to the freedoms that God fearing Americans believe. We must if we are to survive as a nation stand-up against all organizations that profit from division and hate, before they become to powerful and overtake our form of government, and lead us to a destructive path of civil war, and worse.

We who believe in freedom and independence should not fear those who espouse political correctness, but we would be wise to regain a sincere respect for our country's Judeo-Christian heritage and traditions that has guaranteed our prosperity and protection for over 200 years.

Who's Conspiratorial Plan?

Our Constitutional freedoms of speech and religion are under attack from the hyper-sensitive media forces and civil activist groups who do much to promote the notion that evangelicals have a unified conspiratorial plan to elect a fundamentalist apartheid-type of government to rule over every aspect of American life. Casting evangelicals as subversive, conspiratorial members of lobbies that jeopardize the security of America. Oh really! These are baseless and slanderous accusations that cannot be proven, but nonetheless if allowed to repeat the lie long enough; the masses are fooled into believing the lie. These so-called intellectuals make this absurd accusation and for too long now have gotten by with their indoctrination. Christians as a whole believe in the truest intent of our forefathers that we should live in a free and pluralistic society, and that every person should be afforded the right to believe as he chooses without persecution and ridicule. Certainly evangelical Christians take their convictions and values when voting, but don't all people do the very same thing? It's absurd to think that liberals, feminists, gays, abortionists, neo-conservatives, republicans, democrats, and independents do not likewise! We in America are all free people who have a right and obligation to vote our conscience. By maligning evangelicals only and disallowing their right to participate in government is conspiring to create a system controlled by anti-Christian forces, which use minority driven complaints to overrule the majority. Their devious tactics are meant to rule America into some kind of secular nirvana. The anti-Christian bias in this country is wrongheaded and the battle zones are zeroed in on Christians, the 10 commandments, God in the pledge of allegiance, defaming the Boy Scouts, advances in the culture of death through abortion and euthanasia, and attempts to impose homosexual marriage by judicial fiat.

As Christians, we cannot afford to idly stand-by and do nothing, and it is well past-time to take-on the God-haters of this nation, by standing up for truth and not being ashamed to be called Christian. Jesus said, "Do not be surprised that the world hates you, they hated me long before they hated you," (Jn.15:18). May God empower you to make your stand in whatever capacity and role He has called you to, so that His truth may advance. If we don't, we may lose our freedoms of speech and religion in this country.

Was it so long ago that we as American people once trusted in the Judeo-Christian God of Abraham, Isaac, and Jacob? In my humble opinion, it would advance us greatly to go back to our time-tested traditions that made our country great, and put away these foolish notions of political correctness, a flawed morality code, full of inconsistencies promoted by an elitist minority. We the majority who say we believe in God need to be consistent in what we say we believe, because hypocrisy will never lead anyone to God's wonderful truth, that our creator is alive and well, and that he loves all of mankind.

One World Government

The push is strong from a president who is highly motivated to mislead our country into a world government. Did you know that even Walter Cronkite advocated a global government concept. He was awarded a Norma Cousin Global Award, strong proponents of global government. Good ole Walter seemed to be persuaded that this kind of government would best represent what he said, "better justice, peace, and fairness amongst nations." He also said disturbing things like, "we must yield some of our sovereignty as a nation." Walter was a trusted voice for many years, but he was wrong in supporting ideas of global government.

If you trust the scriptures in Genesis 11, this one world government was tried before when prideful men tried to build a tower to heaven, the tower of Babel. A great infrastructure movement and a universal language were adopted, but the triune God had other plans and confused their language and separated them, and thus formed their own distinct nations. Why did God do this? If all the peoples of the world are controlled by one leader, how easy would it be to be deceived into believing a lie? How easy would it be to worship a man or false idol, instead of worshipping the real creator?

Respect for our Judeo-Christian God, respect for our nations sovereignty and governmental system of checks and balances have prospered us and protected us thus far. Why would we want to change the greatest and grandest form of government this world has ever seen?

Divided and Half Free

Abraham Lincoln in his "House Divided" speech told us an eternal truth. "No nation can exist half slave and half free." I submit we are all slaves to the unjust taxes coming from every direction coined cleverly as for some good purpose. Taxes are determined by local, state, and federal laws and many of these laws are unjust. Take real estate taxes for example. Each state is different in the amount they take, so I will share a short story of tax harassment that happened in my life. I purchase some land locked land nearly an acre for a fairly modest price. What I didn't realize at the time was my real estate taxes would go up nearly forty percent the next year. I argued until I was blue in the face that the taxes were unfair. But, the county officials offered no sympathy or help. So I investigated it further and found out that I could appeal. This process took over two years, and the mean while I was paying a ridiculous amount of taxes compared to my neighbors with comparable homes. They argued that the land purchase was zoned residential, but clearly the land was not developed and pasture land with no road access. Still they argued the taxes were fair based on the size of property and value. Well to make a long story a bit shorter, the appeal was partially successful, but I offer no credit to the tax officials and the unjust laws they were enforcing, but something else happened that finally gave me some relief. A small town high school was seriously in debt, and was forced to close. My next year's taxes went down considerably to a more reasonable amount. That painful experience made an indelible mark on me that I will never forget. The first thing that popped into my head was, "I don't really own my property, do I?" Why should I pay real estate taxes in the first place? And why should I have to pay for my house over and over again? Is it to provide for a public school that is totally in the red.? The answer is yes. What if I choose not to have my children attend a public school? It doesn't matter; I would have to pay my unfair share just like everybody else. I wonder if my house would be totally paid for by now if I could have used that tax money to pay down on my home. The answer again would be yes, I could have. Taxes abound today in many ways, from taxes on gasoline for your car, to any purchase you make at a store, and the income tax that is stolen from the money you make. There is also something called a "death tax." Now that is really clever don't you think? Excuse me for dying. I have just scratched the surface of all the tax burdens we face, and I know many of you are fully aware of all the tax obligations. Still, the one that bothers me the most is social security. Many Americans are still convinced that this social program is the most wonderful plan ever devised by a president. That would be the great Franklin D. Roosevelt (Democrat). For the poor who don't have much, or for those who fail to plan very well regardless of income, I guess the overall gist of social security plan could be a good thing. Still, can we really trust the government to save and dole out our money fairly? For one, our government has already spent everything in the social security fund. Yes, social security is one big IOU. The only reason people are getting money today is because we are just going further into debt or printing money with no gold or silver to back it up. And the reason the social security fund is zero is because politicians decided to spend on something more important, according to them. Would you believe that even our social security money is being taxed, yes, even our would-be retirement? The money we worked so hard for must be taxed for the greater collective. That would be our government. No, I meant to say that would be our social government! If we were to average the amount of taxes an average person pays it would be over forty percent of your income. And, the percentage continues to grow every year.

I submit we are all slaves to unjust taxes cleverly manipulated by our by elected officials. But why are so many people passive and hamstrung to do anything? For one, I believe people are not fully engaged or paying attention, and there is way too much blind faith in the political party they choose to support, or they choose to listen to a biased media source that doesn't properly report the truth, who rather gives opinion of a liberal ideology point of view. Also, I believe many are woefully ignorant of our countries history, and why we became a nation. I don't think one has to become a great historian to understand that we broke away from England because King George III decided the colonies were becoming too independent and therefore enacted unjust laws, excessive taxes, and took away individual liberties. And then, little America decided to fight back. One doesn't have to be a genius to figure that out, but so many people think they are powerless to do anything significantly to change Washington, and to keep our liberties alive. I say, we can, and we should! Why should we be alarmed, I say this because Washington is now occupied by someone who thinks he is king.

There are too many programs in our government that are taxing us without fair representation, and as well morally corrupting all of us. Programs like Planned Parenthood which is forced sex education in public schools. And the tax money they get from all of us is used to promote abortion. For many of us who believe this is murder, is it fair that we be forced to support it? There are many other social programs that are too numerous to mention and are grossly mismanaged. Still, I must mention the social welfare program that has proven to be a colossal failure by creating addictions and dependency instead of responsible living.

But by far the biggest government program that has too much freedom to invade our lives is the IRS. This growing monster that Obama decided to grow even more is the most abusive agency ever created and is at war with our freedoms. The IRS has proven to be a harassment agency and has a dubious record of abuses. Tactics of intimidation, especially directed at religious organizations is common. Did you know the IRS can attach a 100% tax on a debtors wage and or property; invade the privacy of a citizen without a court process; can seize property without a court order; can force a citizen into a special IRS court, and subject the citizen to electronic surveillance without a court order? They have also conducted armed searches, and routinely target people with snooping, harassment, and entrapment. As far as I am concerned I think we all would be better off without this government program. Go with something simple like a flat tax rate, therefore eliminating the need for the IRS. I wonder how many billions of dollars we would save by defunding that program? Of course, the IRS doesn't want that to happen so they try to enhance their image, and they continue to justify their reason for existence. Their clever tactic is to allow tax refunds for the poor and some middle class, while hitting the wealthier with most of the tax burden. This is also another way to create class warfare, and covetous attitude. By the way, this is one of the Ten Commandments, "Thou shalt not covet thy neighbor's goods," (10th commandment). Socialism and Communism has entangled itself into the very fabric of our society and it will take strong measures to remove its powerful delusion and influence. There is a growing contingency of young people who are being brainwashed especially by our public schools and universities, the curriculum, and the teachers telling them what to think, instead of how to think, and convincing them that it is okay to receive something free without working for it, so long as it enhances the government in the long run.

I ask a few simple questions. Why do we need the IRS? Why do we need politicians who constantly want to raise taxes and want to create some kind of government that eliminates the God of our fathers? Why do we want to abandon our great Constitution? Has not the God of our fathers inspired the great writings they put together in helping us to becoming a great nation on earth? Citizens of these United States, the IRS is an agency that is operating with excessive powers, with no one holding them accountable. We must support a candidate who see's the wisdom of putting them (government bureaucrats) out of existence, and bringing justice and fairness back to our great land.

Extreme Politics

The conservative leaning citizens of this country, often associated with the Republican Party and Libertarian Party, (although not exclusively conservative), are always demonized as extreme. The most recent uprising of the conservative movement is seen in the Tea Party movement. These good folks do not endorse all Republican Party candidates, no, they are separate and unique "grass movement," peaceful uprising if you will of concerned citizens united under one banner, freedom. Freedom from high taxes and big government, and freedom to worship the God of our fathers. Freedom of peaceful protest like the great Martin Luther King once did, is exactly what they are doing. They alone are truly responsible for the great turnaround of conservative candidates that shook the very foundations of the US Congress. Their passionate gatherings and influence most definitely affects both parties most profoundly. Again, it must be made clear that the Tea Party citizens represent independent and Democrats reportedly at forty percent, and not solely Republican. The Democrat leaders are keen on repeating talking points of propaganda, most recently Senator Schumer was caught on air extolling the virtues of extremism coming from the Tea Party citizens influencing the Republican Party. From that point the Democrat leaders all used the word extreme as a code word in demonizing the Republican Party. This is an old game plan tactic they have used many times before, and will continue to do so long as it benefits them in advancing their political agenda.

In truth, the extremism in politics fit's the Democrat Party. They continue to use old Communistic tactics of blaming their opponents of the very thing they are doing. Deception and dishonesty is at the core of their leadership, thinking that if they can reach their goals of a new world order, or socialism/Marxist nirvana all will be well in their world. Many Democrat voters are not fully aware of their leaders' deception and future goals of changing the American form of government. Many times they speak half truths, or just intentionally lie to the American public. They continue to do this because rarely are they held accountable by the liberal media that fails to report the truth. Too often good Americans are confused with whom to trust, so the blame game goes back and forth. An old saying goes this way, "if a prophet warns of an impending doom, and it doesn't happen, why would you trust that false prophet." People just need to pay attention to what they (politicians) say, and what they do, and if their actions are consistent with their words then respect them with your vote. If their actions are not consistent with their words, why in the world should we trust them with our vote?

Palestinian Flag Over Washington

The facts are as of January 2011, PLO officials hoisted their banner flag at Washington D.C. The PLO mission Chief Maen Areikat said "it's about time that this flag that symbolized the struggle of the Palestinian people for self-determination and statehood be raised in the U.S.." First, let's be clear the Palestinian state has not been created yet. They refuse to negotiate with Israel or accept the existence of Israel.

Representative Ileana Ros-Lehtinen (R-Fl), head of the House Foreign Affairs Committee has said "raising this flag in DC is part of the Palestinian leadership's scheme to manipulate international acceptance and diplomatic recognition of a yet-to-be-created Palestinian state." Israel rejects PA's demand for all the land east of the 1948 Armistice line, so, there is not agreement. This is a clear slap in the face of Israel our ally and friend. Not only is the White House administration implicit with the Palestinian state promotion, but so is Russia and numerous South American countries who support the claim that Arabs own ancient Jewish lands of Samaria and Judea. The Russians say they have supported the independent Palestinian state since Yasser Arafat first declared independence in 1988, said Russian President Dmitry Medvedev. Not soon after the Obama administration allowed the Palestinian flag to be raised in Washington for the first time ever.

Let's also be clear, Yasser Arafat was a terrorist, and Russia supported him. The reason Russia supports terrorists should be clear to all that they want to de-stabilize the region and destroy the nation Israel. The question I ask is why would the Obama administration stand with Russia, and why would they allow a terrorist flag to be flown in Washington? There is much confusion from the liberal media about the Palestinian issue, and they do this intentionally to gain public support, and they do much to undermine Israel's struggle to live in peace. Because they rarely report the truth, they make Israel out to be the enemy with their calculated and biased reporting.

The people named Palestinians are actually poorer Arabs who were gathered from Arab nations and scattered throughout Israel. The Arab leaders did not want them so they intentionally planned this to de-stabilize the region. Israel did take them in and gave them work, and lived in relative peace in Israel. But terrorist organizations like Hama's have threatened these people that they must not live in peace, so many of them have been persuaded to align themselves with the terrorists. They are hiding the fact of their terrorist intentions by claiming they own land in Israel. This is nothing more than a ploy to cover up their real intentions. It is sad that these poorer class Arabs have been manipulated to be Israel's enemies, when they were relatively content to live and work in Israel. Israel's support of these people before they were manipulated by Hama's, was truly an act of kindness.

Reference: Israel My Glory, pg. 40
Israel in the News, Mar/Apr 2011

Social Unrest

Social unrest is occurring at an alarming rate throughout the world. The Arab Spring takeover in Egypt and Libya are prime examples. The Taliban's disturbing influence in causing revolt in Iraq, Afghanistan, and Pakistan is ever present. But the center hub of terrorism is promoted by the radical leaders in Iran. Then you have riots in Great Britain, France, Greece and Italy. The socialism governments of Europe are going broke, and still they refuse to debunk the failed ideology of socialism. There are many wars of attritions in Africa where nations are being split because of Muslim extremism. In the U.S. we are not exempt from the social unrest, and we are in the beginnings of mob protest because of union atrocities that we saw in Madison, Wisconsin because they didn't agree with the Governors' decision. Currently our nation is being attacked from communist/socialist leaders who are actually supporting and promoting the Wall Street protest, and the protests are popping up throughout the nation. These leaders are exploiting the minds of youth, especially those youth who are caught up in the socialism lie that is taught at our universities. Our youth have given their loyalty to these universities to take a curriculum that is not advantageous to finding a good job, and the ever rising costs to go to these universities is another added burden on them as they soon find out the ridiculous amount of debt they incur. So they blame the capitalist idea, or they blame successful businesses, or Wall Street, but the blame should be directed at Washington and the liberal politicians who promote the failed policies of socialism. As well, blame should be directed at liberal professors who demand more money, and the university leadership who promote this kind of propaganda and socialist ideology.

Is there a commonality amongst all this upheaval? In my opinion this unrest is promoted by ungodly people from many directions. I have spoken earlier of all the organizations, politicians, liberal media forces, and George Soros who promote this unrest, but there is something more that should be considered. From the beginning when man was created he bought the lie that God was holding back something and believed

Satan instead of trusting God. Since then man's fallen nature has led him to always want something more, and as much as people do not like to admit it, there is evil in the world. Man has a propensity to blame it on social inequality, or one's environment for their lack of material wants. The nature of man is always seeking satisfaction by obtaining more and more things. Instead they should seek a right relationship with God. Jesus said, "Seek ye first the kingdom of God, and all these things will be added unto you." But it is not man's nature or first priority to seek God, or to do good to one's neighbor. Instead man seeks to gather more whether it is power, or material wealth at the expense of another neighbor. It comes down to this; man has a fallen nature, not un-similar to the fallen angels who were thrown out of heaven who followed the great angel "Lucifer" when he led a rebellion against God. This is the whole reason behind Jesus coming to earth and starting a revolution for truth and his sacrificial death to provide mankind an escape from his fallen nature. Jesus said, "Peace I give to you, not as the world gives." He offers us an internal peace in knowing our creator. This reason alone is why America has prospered because our founding fathers understood what it meant to have a right relationship with their creator. Thus, I believe God helped them to create the Constitutional Articles and Declaration of Independence. There is no doubt their writings reflected their dependence upon God. There was always division amongst the denominations of that period for doctrinal differences, yet they came together for the great cause of freedom.

Sadly in these days we find ourselves in a culture movement that has shook off their dependence on God, and are attempting to do things on their own. Social unrest will continue to grow in America unless we sincerely go back to trusting our Judeo Christian God. Again, be comforted by the words of Jesus in John 14:27, "Peace I leave with you, my peace I give you. I do not give to you as the world gives. Do not let your hearts be troubled and do not be afraid."

Problems with Passivism and Naivety in America

Far too many American people think that everyone in the world wants peace. Far too may are swayed by the old Beatles song "All You Need is Love." Oh really! Wouldn't it be nice to live in such a world? Excuse me for saying so, but a reality awakening is really needed for those who are sleeping in a fantasy world. 911 was a real happening, and we were attacked leaving nearly 3,000 dead. The kind of war we are now engaged in is not the kind of warfare that we are accustomed to, nonetheless, we have enemies out there that want to destroy us by whatever means. It saddens me that a great many folks are jumping on the popular band-wagon in bashing former President Bush for leading us into war, and for interrupting our pampered lifestyle. Certainly as citizens we have the right to question his decisions and how the war is being waged, but to attack him personally and show disrespect to him and to the office only serves to embarrass us and divide us, and lessen the integrity of all of us who call ourselves Americans. Americans are not unified because our grand political parties are more intent on power and control, and quite content to continue acting like dysfunctional children. We are manipulated to take sides because we become indoctrinated from irresponsible media fronts, European countries who embrace socialism, and from civil activist groups who push their agenda.

The reason I am writing this opinion is to try helping those who are relying too much on all the negative media hype, mostly directed at "Mr. Bush" as they like to say, when they should be addressing him with his appropriate title as President Bush.

Muslim extremism is on the rise in not just one country but is spreading to others. Iran is at the heart of the rebellious uprising towards western countries. Ahmadinejad, president of Iran repeatedly declares his intentions to execute genocide on an entire nation. As he has said, Israel the "little Satan," and the United States the "big Satan." It is a grave error to write-off his bellicosity as mere clap-trap coming from a man that may have nuclear means in the very near future. The naïve crowd that is always spouting-off saying all we need to do is negotiate are full of it....or should I say, full of pacifism and naivety. President of Iran can be compared to Adolf Hitler. His denial of history of the holocaust that six million Jews died under Hitler's rule, and ironically there are six million Jews in Israel today! Radical Islam embraces like tactics of Nazism as they indoctrinate their children with hate towards Israelis and Americans, and their continuity of hateful dogma is growing! The influx of Iranian ideology, mosques, and imams who preach their hatred of all things not radically Islamist could indoctrinate millions of Muslims from all over the Arabic world. It has already spread to Syria who was once a people who predominantly followed Christianity, but now less that 10% and these poor folks are in danger of loosing their lives. Syria's Bashar Assad has allowed forty-one Iranian based charities permission to operate in Syria. These use the models of Hezbollah and Hama's during its recent Palestinian conflict with Israel. Syria is rapidly becoming an instrument of Iran to impose hegemony over the entire middle-east as it seeks to establish an Islamic regime that will include Iran, Syria, Lebanon, and possibly Iraq, and eventually the entire region. Diplomacy will never work with terrorists and it will not work with Iran. Negotiations are a nicer way to do things, but we need to wake-up because nice means surrender to them! We can all learn from history if we choose too, but I fear a majority are becoming pacifist like France was before they were conquered by Nazi Germany. As well, the good folks of Germany were too passive when Hitler and Nazism were growing.

Today, the world is much too passive about terrorism. Former President George Bush, to his credit has warned us about the global caliphate is not far away, and I agree with him that we need to confront terrorism now!! Further, let us not be ignorant of Russia who is a major supplier of technology to create nuclear advancement in Iran. Russia has also been consistent with blocking efforts to impose UN sanctions on Iran.

So, what does all of this tell you? Do you really know who your enemy is, or are you so focused on dividing America into two political camps that you're unable to see the enemy right in front of you? God help us. A note worth remembering is that according to the Constitution our government's main responsibility is to protect us, the American citizen. I hope the good citizens of this nation will rise-up and vote for the right person who will prioritize protecting our country and leading our people to higher morale ground which hopefully would incur the blessings of our heavenly creator. May we support the kind of president who is empathetic to its citizens and to the cause of freedom. Someone with enormous amounts of money, charisma, a pretty smile and popularity is not required!

CHAPTER 5

PRETENDER POLITICS

*I*f you say you are conservative, be a conservative. Don't be a "glass half-full." An old quote from the Bible says, "I'd rather have you hot or cold, but not luke-warm." Because luke-warm means" I'd rather spit you out of my mouth." This paraphrase expresses God's attitude towards his followers who lack zeal. Practically speaking about the drinks we drink, it is either hot or cold that satisfies our taste buds, but never do we like a luke-warm drink. So I draw the conclusion that politics is no different. If Republicans think they want to be reasonable or non-offensive, and promote candidates that have temperatures of "luke-warm," I say no thanks. Liberal to moderate candidates who masquerade themselves as conservatives are exactly the problem. A true conservative can be best described as one who first follows the Constitution as it written by our founders, second, one who believes in smaller government and lower taxes, and third, one who respects life and the creator God who gives life. These three pillars are the very basic foundation of what I believe is conservative. All other definitions of what may be branded conservative are false, or what we would call liberalism. This definition does not necessarily coincide with one particular political party. In short, just because one may have a Republican label does not mean they are truly conservative. So as a responsible voter we must know who we are voting for, and would discourage voting one party line. I do however believe there are more conservative candidates or incumbents that are Republican that there are Democrats. Obviously Democrats are more united in their progressive socialism convictions, but there are many Republicans who masquerade as conservative but are really more liberal. If we as Americans want a positive change in government we must consider voting for conservative politicians. This responsibility falls on voters to vote responsibly and take power from party influences and manipulation. Because so many people are not paying attention to the kind of elected officials that have invaded our government, we are in danger of losing our form of government. This is why we must be vigilant in supporting "Tea Party" candidates. It is important to remember this statistic; forty percent are Democrats and independent voters who are active in the "Tea Party" movement. Many who voted for Mr. Obama are now disillusioned by arbitrate and despotic control our government is attempting to force upon the American people. We must stand together to create responsible governing and respect for our great Constitution. A true conservative gives us the best hope to reach this goal.

The Republican Party needs to solidify itself behind the conservative movement because the "Tea Party" alone should be credited for the grass movement and exciting people and activism against liberalism. If they choose not to support real conservative's they do so at their own peril. A lot of folks out there are really upset, and they will vote on November 2nd. Politics "as usual" will not satisfy the voter this year, so the elites in both parties better wake-up. Carl Rove, Krauthammer and others who are Republicans who are criticizing "Tea Party" candidates only look at controlling the House and Congress, but what good would that be if they are liberal who do not support conservative policies? It would only discourage the peoples trust in the Republican Party, as it has already done. Criticism of Ronald Reagan was that he was too conservative. Yet, he became our greatest conservative president in the past decade. All too often the "big tent" idea is too dangerous because it engrafts too many liberals. I believe moderates if left with a choice between Marxist liberals and strong conservatives will overwhelmingly choose the "right." This is how Ronald Reagan won, and he unified the party. This is the winning strategy that will win today. Let us not waver or become "wishy-washy" or "lukewarm," because the people are likely to "spit you out!"

The Party Is Over

As Americans maybe it is time to do something about the two big parties "gone wild." Yes, I am talking about the Democrats and the Republicans. Call me radical, but I'd much rather live without either of these parties dictating to us who we need to vote for, and what we need to vote for. They have too much power and influence, too much media bias, and too much money! The Democrats are being controlled more and more by powerful people and groups who are advocating social global governance with government ruling over us like a tyrannical king. They still fool many people into thinking that they are friends to the poor and middle-class with failed social programs, and they are excellent at creating class-warfare and diverting their failures upon the rich and wealthy. Big money and big companies are their scapegoat refusing to admit their mistakes to the American people, and they continue to lie and misrepresent the truth. I believe this political party has done more to cripple and harm this country than any other party! Now don't think for a minute that I am excusing the Republican Party because I am not. They are basically too aloof to condescend to the poor because of their addiction to money and to power. They believe in capitalism and trickle-down economics and it has become their god, but many fail to see compassion. People do not trust them because so many in their party are no different than the Democrats. They want their power and they want their way come hell or high water! But they are not united as well in sending a well tune message to the American people to their detriment, but in some ways it is a good thing because many Republicans are independent thinkers and entrepreneurs. Many Republicans claim to be conservative, who honor God and family, and country. Many Democrats claim to be liberal, who honor God and family, and country. Moderates seem to mingle amongst both. All I can say for sure is that there are some good out there that love God and country, but there are an increasing number of folks who hate our country and form of government, and there are some who want everything for free. I want to be clear and make distinction. There are many good Democrats and many good Republicans out there who really love to be called an American, who love this country and would fight to save this free Republic. But the problem as I see it is that Americans have too much blind trust in these parties who claim to represent the people. These parties rank with hypocrisy. They say one thing and do another, all the time!!! Some try to blame our form of government because there are so many hoops to jump through, our founders would call it "checks and balances." People like George Soro's who organized "Move On.Org" a big fundraiser of the Democrat Party, and one who actually advocates the overthrow of our form of government, is in fact pushing the global government ideology, and national socialism. National Socialism was the government that ruled Nazi Germany. It was an efficient kind of government because Hitler was a dictator. Nobody dared to argue with him, and he got things done. So for the sake of argument he was efficient and he accomplished much in his hate filled march to fascism. His charisma was intoxicating and inspiring and the people followed his hellish dreams that led to the demise and destruction of the Hebrew community and his own Germanic people. I wouldn't call that success no matter how efficient he got things done would you?

The parties have been ruling us for too long, and the "big" factor is the problem. When an organization or government becomes too big and too powerful, who puts the "checks and balances" on them?

It basically comes down to trust. Who do you trust? Nobody likes to be told what to do, nobody likes their freedom taken away. So do you trust government to be your god and supplier of everything, and of course they would own you and your property; or would you rather be independent and own your own property and have the freedom to choose whether you believe and trust in the real God?

"Trust in the Lord with all of your heart, and lean not to your own understanding but in all your ways acknowledge Him, and He will direct your paths." (Proverbs 3:5-6)

Party Corruption

From the land of Lincoln honesty is not something we Illinoisans' see much of nowadays, and we have seen grand examples of political corruption from both parties. Recently, Governor Blagovich always mentions Rom Immanuel that he brokered the selling of the Illinois Senate seat, and according to him an investigation into Rom Immanuel's involvement would help exonerate him. The Governor's lawyers want to subpoena Rom Immanuel and President Obama. No doubt our beleaguered Governor wants to free himself from guilt, but if this should ever happen it would be interesting justice to see Chicago politics a bit exposed. The White House is trying to protect the president, but if he is involved no president should be exempt from testifying in a court of law. We should never forget that we are a government of laws, and no one should be above it, not matter what their position.

Senator Burris was appointed to the vacant senate seat by Governor Blagovich, and was not even voted in by the people of Illinois. Governor Quinn was also appointed to office after Mr. Blagovich was removed; again he also was given the office without being voted in by the people. To me this is just a convenient way to sidetrack the will of citizens. For any politician to be appointed to a seat without being voted in by the people is an unjust law and is not Constitutional. When a political party can make up laws to enhance their power base it leads to corruption because the will of the people is not represented, and their voice is diminished. Another example of this kind of corruption is when the two major political parties can prevent a fair debate by preventing other candidates to participate who may be an independent or from a different party. Political parties should never have that kind of power or influence.

As a voter we must become more educated and engaged in the voting process. How many times must we go to the polling place and not be fully informed on whom we are voting for? Just because we lean towards one party more than the other does not mean we should blindly vote strictly on party lines. This is voting in ignorance and trusting in a party solely without any personal investigation. In today's politics we have incumbents and candidates who masquerade themselves as someone they are not. During the Republican candidate race of recent we had Democrats register as Republicans to cast their vote for McCain because they didn't want a more conservative candidate to win the nomination. This kind of thing is voter fraud and leads to manipulating the voting process, and corrupting the will of the people. The truth is that Republicans decided to do the same thing in response to what the Democrats did previously. More often than not, many liberals will do anything to win. Many liberals masquerade as conservatives or moderates, and the people are fooled into voting for someone with whom they really don't agree with. What is needed to ensure integrity in the process is a bi-partisan group that offers report cards of incumbents and candidates on what issues they stand for, and what they have supported as an incumbent, or what new candidates are promising. We need to support an independent group that provides flyers and internet report cards on all politicians. This kind of information (report cards) must be available and provided to the people before elections, and at the polling place. It is true that some people are more engaged and informed, but I dare say that the majority of voters are not well informed on whom they are voting for, regardless if they are local, state or on a federal level. We must as good citizen's vote for an individual who most aligns with our values and beliefs, and we need to support those people who uphold the Constitution. I also believe that many people have been indoctrinated into believing in a perverted social justice pushed on society by socialists/progressives who are growing in number especially among our youth. This is because socialism is being taught in our schools and especially in our universities where they have more freedom to indoctrinate unsuspecting minds. College professors often paint socialism as some kind of utopia, but it really just steals wealth from the ambitious workers and inventors of prosperity to a class of people who do not want to work, or who feel they are owed to some kind of entitlement. This only instills resentment and disunity in society. Socialism also teaches against capitalism, which in my mind would kill the resourceful spirit of an individual who wants to grow a business. Socialism encourages a large state to control the masses where an elite few govern. They will always generate class warfare, so in their minds they hope to keep everybody in a cage, everybody making the same meager wage, everybody working for the enhancement of the government. One could call it socialism, communism, fascism, collectivism, but whatever it is, I call it tyranny and oppressive to anybody who wants to be free. We have so many misguided people jumping up and down demanding what they think is their right. Things that are not in the Constitution like health care, rights to be given a home without having any obligation to pay for it, and unjust laws to provide for illegal aliens health care when they haven't paid a dime in taxes, and to top it off they are not even legal citizens. Excuse me for saying so, but it sure seems like Obama wants to bankrupt America. He is always claiming some kind of crisis to kind of camouflage his real intent to change our form of government. Some conservative radio hosts claim that all the bailout money, buying GM and other car companies, Fannie Mae and Freddie Mac disaster, stimulus money schemes are all done intentionally by the government, growing an immense debt in an attempt to destroy capitalism, and creating a perfect moment to introduce socialism to America.

People need to be educated on the truest intents of what our Constitution means. This means as "Constitutionalists" we need more effort to inform the American people, and we must do this locally. Local government will free people into a better understanding to vote for the right candidate at the polling place. We must free ourselves from the blind support of party allegiance. Blind faith in one political party, Constitutional ignorance, voting apathy, and throwing God out of our lives, are by far the biggest problems we face in America. We must try to free people from ignorance in helping them to understand our founding fathers principles, and learn an appreciation for their passion, sacrifice, and vision for America.

Moderate Compromise

If politicians want to be identified as conservative they need to stand firm on what they claim. Wishy-washy moderate politicians never seem to find what they really believe, and all too often are not honest with the American people who support them. To me, these kinds of politicians are all about their own advancement and less determined about representing people. The American people have spoken loudly in the Tea Party. They want less government, and they want fewer taxes, and they want politicians to go back to the Constitution. In evaluating the GOP debates you hear the argument from the "old Republican guard" who are mostly moderate Republicans and not purely conservative. They say," We need to pick the candidate that can best defeat Obama." This sound bite came from Chris Christy, governor of New Jersey, who is throwing his support for Mitt Romney. He says Romney has the most experience in the public and private sector, and is the one who can best defeat Obama. He has a right to his opinion, but I for one am looking for candidate who has the best experience of representing conservative principles. Someone who is like Ronald Reagan who was an unapologetic hard core conservative; who by the way won in a landslide. I do not see that coming from Mitt Romney who has flip-flopped on abortion, and created a state health care plan that was a big beauracracy not un-similar to the Obama health care plan. In fact, Romney's aids went to the White House on several occasions to help give advice to those creating the Obama health care plan. Romney is all about economics, and less concerned on really pushing conservative values; in my opinion. We can do better, and we don't have too compromise and give in to scare tactics to eliminate truly conservative candidates. The candidates we should look to support are the ones who have a vision to fix America's problems. Liberalism promotes the weedy invasion of socialism attacking the foundational pillar of faith of our Constitution. The socialism invasion pushed at our universities is corrupting our youth, who do not have a clear understanding of our countries history. We must do more to win the hearts and minds of our youth if we want to win the cultural war within our country. The socialism invasion has over the years choked the great writings of our Constitution into ineffectiveness and confusion. It arises in the Judiciary branch and the Legislative branch, and Congress. Newt Gingerich made it clear in one of his addresses on CSPAN describing problems with the judiciary branch in how they have become dictatorial in attempting to silence the speech and religious rights of Americans. He says in short, the Congress and the President have the power to supersede a judge's decision, and can actually remove a judge from their post. When a judge goes outside our Constitutional boundaries it is the legislative branch and the President responsibility to act. This is a great comment from Newt, and we need to do this to curb the judicial activism that is corrupting our land.

We have in the past been asleep and not paying attention to the subtle attacks from socialists. Too much compromise has been the problem for years, and we must take America back to its original roots. Governor Perry has a book that warns us about the problems with the federal government and thus he has enacted state laws to fight back. He has fought back by eliminating a government program of Planned Parenthood in his state. That's a good thing, and is exactly the kind of action we expect from a conservative president. This abhorrent program strikes at the heart and values of a human beings worth, and I applaud his decision. We desperately need a candidate who will fight back against intrusive government, and we need to support one who understands the great value of our Constitution and liberties, and one who will protect us from socialists and their unjust laws. Our media outlets are shortsighted in seeing the big picture when they only look at economic issues. Blessings that come from God are not just economic prosperity. But, I believe economic prosperity will come when we embrace the whole picture of valuing human life. The

Declaration of Independence reminder is "We are endowed from our creator with certain inalienable rights of life, liberty, and property (pursuit of happiness)." We must never let government take the place of God, because only God can give contentment and blessing, and free a soul to live a godly and purposeful life.

CHAPTER 6

ARTICLES OF CONCERN

Why On Earth?

ave you asked yourself why our government is a safe haven for liars and thieves? I believe our Constitution was created by great men whose influence has led our country into greatness, but we have forgotten the great words of Benjamin Franklin who said, "Elected officials go to a post of honor, not a place of profit." Do we not as American citizens bear responsibility for who we vote in office? Even our system of checks and balances has been subverted and twisted into ineffectiveness. Truth is rarely reported within our major media outlets, and they do everything possible to support their liberal friends. Academia has become a propaganda house of education as well. Communism and Marxist thought is alive and well in America, and questionable organizations like the ACLU, Acorn, Planned Parenthood and a host of others are allowed to subsist and advance on our tax dollars. Elections are being stolen not dissimilar the election tyranny in Iran. Conservative thought is branded as extreme, and capitalism is labeled as evil. Our military is not honored, and our nation's sovereignty is not protected, and God is removed by treasonous judges. Politicians strut around doing their business stealing American jobs and giving them to foreigners who do all they can to add power to themselves and their party while ignoring its citizens. In less than sixty days our president gave us trillions of dollars in debt from unconstitutional bailouts and takeovers, and now pushing a cap and trade bill. The largest and most expensive in our nation's history. If my memory serves me correctly, our president said "no new taxes on the lower and middle class."

Why on God's green earth would we want to allow ourselves to be led down destructive paths that will not bless or prosper our nation? In my humble opinion, until we elect the right people in office who respect our Constitution and Judeo-Christian heritage our nation will not get better, but worse. A day is coming when justice will prevail, but my faith reminds me it won't be solely through human intervention.

Cap & Tax

Actually, the bill was called "Cap and Trade," but this is nothing more than clever language coming from politicians using deception to misguide the public. Deception has always been a part of their game plan and it works on Americans who are not well informed or paying attention. I called my congressmen's office to voice my opinion, and attempt to find out how he was going to vote. No clear answers were given. I doubt if even our congressmen know all that is being pushed through especially when an additional three-hundred pages was added on the very day the vote was tallied. Disturbing don't you think? Congressmen and senators are supposed to be our representatives, but they get away with making it difficult to contact them, and are not held accountable. Well, the bill did pass narrowly, and now it goes to the senate for a final vote.

Concerning the bill, those supporting it say it will only raise taxes a few hundred dollars, but those opposed say it will be 3,000 plus a year, and now our growing government wants more of our hard-earned cash. Did not our president promise our taxes wouldn't go up one penny? I don't know how anyone can be happy with this theft, and I don't care how any politician couches support for the bill. The EPA will grow even more to regulate how much CO_2 we can exhale!

First and foremost, do not forget those politicians who vote yes for this bill. The biggest tax proposal in history and the biggest lie. It's all crap, so let us put a lid on it, and flush!!!

Illogical

Why do government officials grant aliens business perks like not paying taxes or putting into the social security fund? Why allow an alien to operate a business in America at all? Have you noticed many small businesses such as gas stations, motels, and grocery stores are now owned by foreigners. Their seems to be a movement by politicians and big business and banks to internationalize America. Many foreigners are buying up property and large businesses such as Dubai and others.

There is a danger of losing our quality of life, especially for those of us who fall into the category of lower to middle-class. The outsourcing movement overseas and cheap labor practices are very evident. Unless a great outpouring of American patriots lift their voices and demand a change in direction, we will lose our way of life, and our ability to prosper or own property. Our nation's greatest challenge to our government and business owners is to love money less, and to love their neighbors more, and to do more to defend America's sovereignty and freedoms. This wake-up call should cause alarm to every American, because we need to be wise on whom we elect as our next president, governor, congressman, senator, representative and local officials. Because, either they are for us as one nation under God with liberties and justice; or they are against us.

Let us stop being naïve and apathetic, because we need to now get involved more than ever and change America for the good, protecting traditional values of family that made us great, and not this phony new morality code of diversity, and this movement of giving away America to foreigners. If our founding fathers thought it wise to protect our nation's sovereignty and to trust in the Judeo-Christian God, who has been faithful to us and blessed us all these years, why now should we abandon this great truth for something that endangers our prosperity and quality of life? Clearly, a movement to a world government is not a hoax, and if you are voting for officials who promote this idea, you're demeaning your quality of life. Captain Kirk's best friend Spock would say, "that's illogical!"

Teachable Moment

Our president says the Cambridge police incident is a "teachable moment for us." Makes me wonder who is "us" that he is referring too? The black professor Gates, who was confronted by a white police officer, is claiming racial profiling. The officer responded to a responsible person's observation that professor Gates was attempting to break into what turned out to be his own house. Apparently he didn't have his key, so when the officer approached him he asked for identification, (standard operating procedure). The professor was verbally loud and abusive, and uncooperative and refused to follow the officer's directions. Accusing the officer of racial motivation, an officer of 15 years service without incident. The professor was arrested for a brief period until he finally cooperated by giving proper identification. Regrettable yes, but who is to blame? I think if professor Gates would have cooperated with the officer their would have been no problem, but he didn't, and the evidence is clear that he escalated the problem. There is also evidence as to why these kinds of incidents happen. Hate organizations that indoctrinate people into thinking that special treatment are owed to them only enhances disunity and anger amongst all Americans regardless of color. These organizations always have an axe to grind on racism, and of course they profit. Racism and greed affects all people, and it is not confined to only one race, and when it happens we as Americans need to expose the hate. Policemen are not perfect all the time, but most of the time they do an invaluable service to all of us by keeping law and order.

Our president fueled the fire by saying the policeman acted stupidly. Kudos to the police department for standing up to the president's accusation and bias. The best teachable moment for America is for President Obama and Professor Gates to apologize to the police department and the police officer. And, may I ask what good will come from having a beer together if no apology is given?

High Court Treason

The Supreme Court is the highest court system in our nation, and these chosen few are appointed for life. What can I do as a citizen when they fail to uphold our form of government? What if they go against our Constitution and attempt to form a different kind of government? Who stands as their judge? What if, for instance, they cater to a socialist system of government? Or totalitarian ideas where they impose the significance of state rule over respect for individual rights afforded to us by the Constitution? What if their service and sole existence is to eradicate all Judeo-Christian influence in our society? Who stands in the gap?

This whole notion of "separation of church and state" is wrongly interpreted by too many judges, who appear to be in lock-step with the ACLU civil activists who promote a purely secular society. In fact, it was an activist judge in the late 1940's who promoted this poisonous doctrine that people of faith should be separated from public office and schools. Thomas Jefferson's quote, although not in the Constitution, was solely intended to mean that no one particular church would rule our government. However, it was never intended to mean that people of faith be excluded from serving or having influence in our government or be excluded from teaching or having influence in our schools.

Our government was built to have checks and balances so that no one branch of government would impose too much power, but that is exactly what has happened because our court systems at all levels are permeated with social activist judges who are making laws instead of interpreting Constitutional laws correctly. These are treasonous acts that should not be tolerated. Doesn't our Constitution direct us as responsible citizens to remove such judges who corrupt our laws?

Iran and Us

As we look from afar at the beginnings of a revolution in Iran I wish we as Americans would be so bold to protest against our crazy out-of-control government. What's different about the Iranians and Americans is not as much as one would think. Yes, Iran is not really a democracy and republic as we are, but they yearn for justice and a righteous government to respect and treat them fairly. They clearly know the voting was manipulated for Aminajab and the Mullahs. The fanatical leaders fear what they think is excessive freedom. They claim they know God, but they know nothing of God. The true God does not prohibit freedoms of speech, freedoms of religion, nor freedoms for women. This God instilled freedom resides in every human being. Iran's leaders struggle to know how to control their people, except by excessive force and murder. What's interesting is that Aminajab's administration use similar tactics not much different from American politicians. They offer gifts to the extreme poor to control their vote, and don't tell their people where they get the money, which is usually stolen. Sounds pretty similar to the slimy tactics we have all seen before to gain votes. Just look at what both parties do to gain illegal aliens vote. Free health care and free access to our country and taking jobs away from legal Americans. Sadly, our government leaders fear freedom just as much as the fanatical religious leaders in Iran. If we do not pay attention to our diminishing freedoms and do not vote for the right people in public office to represent us, precious God-given freedoms such as independence, life, liberty, and the pursuit of happiness will erode and dissolve, coming from an oppressive government that is desperately fearful of freedom and liberty.

Small Tent

People today are discouraged with water-downed politics and little choice. To me, separating the two great parties into specific camps truly would represent the ideals of voters. Something along the lines of liberal-moderate-conservative branches for each party, and let's put an end to the "big tent" notion! Too often all we get is lip service to what they say or promise, and because of their lack of conviction because they don't really believe in what the voter wants, they only say what the voter wants to hear.

Separating the powers into smaller camps would help eliminate elitist powers into something more genuine and representative. Why should we as citizens be limited to just "rich" candidates? Poor Abe Lincoln wouldn't have a chance in our world! Candidates from other parties should also have the same privileges as a Republican or Democrat. Obviously the primary system would have to be re-vamped and organized. The electoral voting system as it is now is unfair. When one candidate receives all the electoral votes from a state, even if they only win marginally? How does that represent people fairly? Let's figure-out a way to stop corrupting politics by reducing the unfair influence of power and wealth.

Ben Franklin said, "There are two passions which have a powerful influence on the affairs of men. These are ambition and avarice; the love of power, and the love of money." He believed that politicians go to a post-of-honor, not a place of profit!!

So Long Freedom!

So long as government continues to grow bigger and we put our faith in state programs taxes will get higher. So long as we allow elitist groups to promote "political correctness" and dictate to us what is acceptable and what is not acceptable, justice and majority rule suffers. So long as we ignore the injustice of "eminent domain" promoted by corrupt officials we diminish individual rights and freedoms guaranteed to us by the Constitution. So long as we ignore the voting process do not be surprised at the outcome or complain when America loses its sovereignty, and the Constitution will be re-written by secular progressives.

Look, we still have a voice in America and your voice counts, because one vote united with millions is powerful. So many trends of injustice going on nowadays, I fear personal ownership will be a thing of the past, because everything will be owned by the state. Totalitarian socialism promotes the idea that progress of the state trumps individual rights. Disturbing trends by city and county officials raising real-estate taxes at their whim, and corrupt judges allowing the stealing of one's property through what's called "eminent domain" is wrong-headed.

Originally, our Constitution was designed to enhance a government for the people not for people to suffer to enhance the government. Ben Franklin warned us that we would become a tyrannical monarchy if we allowed the elite and powerful to control us. Two passions control these types "ambition and avarice; the love of power, and the love of money." He emphasized that "politicians go to a post of honor, not a place of profit." When we decide that selfish love for money and things is more important than respect for our neighbors, then do not be surprised at the level of corruption at all levels!

Hope Misplaced

For centuries people have searched for hope in all the wrong places. They first become disillusioned by believing the lie that life is only a one time happening. That of course eliminates any future life in spirit form, or any God who judges or rewards. Then they believe the lie that humans are basically good. They feel a little enlightenment and good works through human philosophies, or progressive humanism, or man-made religions is all they need. History tells a bleak story of nations who trusted horrific kings and leaders. Especially those who convinced themselves and others that they were gods with divine powers. So, they just come up with their own rules. We have the same thing going on today, replacing God with a man figure, and trusting an ever growing government that will provide everyone's needs. Sadly, these are all "failed policies of the past."

In today's world we hear a lot about hope and change, and the not so subtle message is that a charismatic leader and big government can do this for you. Friends, leave the hope and change department to a proven winner and someone who keeps his promises. "In God We Trust." Our forefathers led us by their words to the great hope of trusting God with our future, not solely money, and not solely government.

What's Wrong with Big Government?

Many American's are beginning to awaken and question our current administrations push for big government, and the notion that going further in debt will solve our problems. Whether it is free health-care or free something else. All of this free stuff has to come from somewhere, and once all the rich folks have been fleeced into oblivion what incentive will they have to produce jobs? Socialism and totalitarian regimes in all their forms have always promoted the idea that the "state" trumps the importance of an individual person. And, if allowed to rule in America our Constitution will have to be re-written. No longer will we enjoy inalienable rights to pursue happiness in ownership of property, because eventually everything will be owned by government. No longer will the individual have freedom of speech, freedom of religion, or freedom to bear arms to protect us from an obtrusive government.

Thus, an atheistic government becomes our god, and worship to its system and its elitist leaders will not be an option. A pastor once said, "Friend, you cannot legislate the poor into freedom by legislating the wealthy out of freedom. And what one person receives without working for, another person must work for without receiving. The government cannot give to anybody anything that the government does not first take from somebody..."

Never forget, our founding fathers were men of faith in the Judeo-Christian God, and they designed our Constitution on the basis of that faith. But never did they envision having faith in big government, and to their credit they warned us against its dangerous powers.

Extreme Bias

American's who are labeled "right-wing" and Muslim terrorists are lumped into one in the same according to our misguided left-wing media outlets. In other words, conservative leaning American's who believe in values such as pro-life, traditional family values, faith in a Judeo-Christian God, small government and capitalism, securing American borders, beliefs in our Constitution as it was written and intended by our forefathers are guilty of right-wing extremism. Interestingly, you don't hear much about left-wing extremism as we should. Left-wing people who espouse values and support things like pro-abortion, gay marriage, atheism, questionable organizations like Acorn and the ACLU, a weak military, big government and socialism, and a promotion of judges who desire to re-write our Constitution. Which by the way, threatens our way of life, where freedoms of speech, freedoms of religion (especially Christianity), and rights to bear arms are labeled as extreme.

As American's we will not agree on every issue, but we should agree on the freedoms we enjoy, but not use excessive freedom to destroy God-given rights to life, liberty and individual freedoms. So as you evaluate the values of the political right and left, honestly ask yourself which side is extreme? We should be careful how we label someone because none of us like to be put into a box, but that's what our government and politicians and so-called media experts try to do, to propagandize and belittle or silence people with whom they disagree. It is time to stand-up on the right side, and do some clear thinking about what's really extreme!

Yes We Can

Yes we can learn from history if we choose to, and we can see the disturbing trend that history has a way of repeating itself. Governments that have been swayed to adopt variations of socialism in the past have proven to be failures. Nazi Germany was led by a mad-man who adopted a government of National Socialism. A leader with great oratory and one who offered great hope and prosperity. America on the other hand was led by a bunch of rag-time dreamers who defeated the greatest military of that period and dawned the idea of small government and the crazy notion of individual freedoms in areas of religion, speech (press), property rights, and minimal tax burdens. They hoped for a government with checks and balances occupied by men of faith in three distinct branches of government; judicial, electoral and legislative. Yet, somehow today we have allowed an illegitimate fourth branch. A gang of atheistic powers who want to change our Constitution and nation. Especially, changing our forefathers writings and proclamation that we are "one nation under God."

Helmer Von Campe, former member of Hitler Youth, now a

loyal American and founder of Truth and Freedom said, "America is witnessing a repeat performance of the tragedy of 1933 when an entire nation (Germany) let itself be led like a lamb to the socialist slaughter-house." Today, we can choose the path for America and the kind of government we want, our current secular humanist worldview without our traditional Judeo-Christian God, or the old proven road our forefathers chose. You know that old road that led us to greatness!

Give Me Liberty

Patrick Henry once said, "give me liberty or give me death," when he fought against British tyranny. God honored his passion and conviction and gave him and his fellow patriot's victory. Today, we need to regain that same kind of passion when freedoms are threatened, and at the voting booth we better be careful who we elect to protect our liberties. The greatest gift our founding fathers gave us are freedoms of speech and the free choice to worship without state or government intervention telling us what is appropriate. Our founding fathers also gave us a Judeo-Christian heritage, and the evidence is undeniable. It is my strong conviction that any judge or politician who cowers to the arguments of the (ACLU) crowd, and radical secular socialists are actually behaving like traitors to our country and attempting to subvert our Constitution.

Friends, are you not fed-up with elitist minority groups promoting their disturbing un-moral code of political correctness and diversity, and their dirty business of rationing free speech? Even broadcasters are threatened, especially conservative talk-radio personalities. Left leaning politician bureaucrats are attempting to impose their so-called "fairness doctrine," which is nothing more than an attempt to restrict journalistic freedom of broadcasters. They realize this freedom of speech is the most potent force for conservative expression in America. This crucial freedom of expression no-matter what persuasion, makes it impossible for a single school of thought in swaying public opinion. Friends, we all have our peculiar belief system about life and values, and we should all try to respect each other, but that doesn't mean we should abandon our convictions and forfeit our great heritage that helped make this country great.

Fair Tax & Less Exploitation

Simply stated, Americans are being exploited by foreigners and big business controlled by an even bigger government. Schemes to promote a global economy and a world government are a possibility. Have you ever wondered why on many products we buy, foreign languages are included on instructional manuals? What ever happened to American products? Instead we mostly get Chinese, Taiwan, Pakistani or Bangladesh! Gullible citizens like me purchase it without realizing its effects. Certainly, we shouldn't exclude our government officials who promote this movement of outsourcing to foreigners. We need to insure that all politicians stop this invasion, or give them the boot! It seems to me they are more intent on giving themselves a raise, and maintaining their power-base than representing the voice of working people. What's needed is downsizing government to be less intrusive, and fewer bureaucrats. Goodbye IRS! Hello flat tax. Forms of consumption tax make sense to promote fairness and reduce property taxes. Stop rewarding aliens who start businesses who don't pay taxes. Start helping true Americans in small business. Next election, please support a candidate who has this vision, and if they fail to see this truth and represent you adequately, simply put pressure on them to change or remove them out of office.

The problem I see is everything is getting too big, whether it is government, oil, utilities, corporate farms, or merchandisers like Wal-Mart. Big doesn't mean better. The trend of "too big" means it intrudes into our lives like socialism does, or in case of big business they monopolize the market and competition because of volume and cheap labor. Foreigners fit into this scheme quite nicely. Unfair labor practices, greedy contractors, outsourcing overseas, alien invasions from Mexico are all disturbing trends of greed, and voter manipulation. Most of us citizens are lower to middle-class workers. We need representation, and we need to vote!

Since the 1940's our taxes have progressively grown from an average of 12% to over 40%, and we can thank our progressive politicians on both sides of the isle for this socialist invasion. To me, lowering taxes for everybody will spur the economy faster than bailing out big companies and putting our country trillions of dollars in debt. Flat taxes and consumer tax with no loopholes are a much fairer way for Americans. Remember, we are not citizens of the world; we are citizens of the United States. If we want to protect our freedoms of speech and religion, the right to have a home and to prosper we must protect the values we hold dear. We must not be lured into thinking that big government will provide everything for you. Because if you do, then they own you and your freedoms are gone. Relying on big government does nothing but destroy your human spirit and hampers the gifts and abilities you were given. I've seen it first hand when people sell their souls to socialist programs and handouts, and it isn't pretty. People lose their incentive to do anything. Remember, big government has never and will never replace God or give you hope.

All Good Men....Come to the Aide of your Fellow Man

Eight men that belong to a Michigan Christian Militia group are in my opinion being targeted as terrorists by the Obama administration. Until they are actually proven to be a serious threat which I greatly doubt, they should be defended by all good people who love American freedoms. This is nothing more than an attempt to silence speech, and an overreaction to control gun rights afforded to all of us under

DREAMS FROM OUR FATHERS

the Constitution. This government invasion on eight militiamen who meet together to have a little fun, are now labeled as radical terrorists. It is curious to me why our government is focused on such a small insignificant group, and not targeting Muslim militia groups who are well established and growing right here in our own country? These Muslim groups are using automatic weapons, IED's and other various explosive devices, but for some reason they are not targeted as possible threats to our nation. Have you ever wondered why our government is not focused effectively on stopping the violence and terrorism from the Mexican drug cartels? Just recently an Arizona rancher was brutally murdered by a member of the Mexican cartel, and the threat is growing. Kidnappings are becoming common place in America, especially troubling in Phoenix Arizona. Reports verify the drug cartels are growing in numbers and in wealth. Some expert's project the cartels have a force of nearly 100,000, who are heavily armed with modern weaponry. Currently the Mexican army has a meager force of 75,000 troops. Sounds pretty dire doesn't it, and the Obama administration is worried about eight Christian militiamen?! Really.

Whether or not you agree with the militia's activities, they are within the law, and the law is clear, "innocent until proven guilty." We would be wise not to believe everything a liberal media is propagating as truth. To me, it is all political maneuvering to establish the impression that they are radical because they are Christian, and using guns. Remember what Obama said in Ohio during his campaign, "desperate people clinging to their guns and Bibles."

Even the accusation the militiamen plotted to harm policemen has not been established. Residents of the area that know the accused say they were active in supporting the local police with fundraisers and various activities.

Our government is totally inconsistent and more concerned about political points in their targeting a patriotic group. Traditional militia groups are established throughout our nation, and have a good history that goes back to the Revolutionary War, and were vital in winning our independence. Is it coincidence that conservative movements such as tea party members are being targeted as being violent? Efforts in the liberal media and liberal politicians have been relentless in their wild accusations. The truth is they are concerned that tea party members who comprise of 40% independents and democrats are active in the tea party effort. Tea party movement is a "grass movement" and is truly bi-partisan, and they are not violent in any credible capacity. They are good Americans who are peacefully protesting the growth of government, government healthcare, and the intrusion on individual and state rights, and they are rallying to preserve American freedoms. Rally On!!!!

In Child-like Faith

In response to an article in our local newspaper (Teach Religious Beliefs in Church, not school), I just have to respond in kind. I agree, church is known as a good place to learn about God, but school can be a good place too. For young people this is their proving ground. Public schools today are really biased because in throwing God out, they now incorporate organizations like Planned Parenthood, and belief systems of New Age and Mother Earth, and other belief systems contrary to Judeo-Christian beliefs. They have fallen victim to the ACLU mantra of atheism, and the false notion of "separation of church and state." (KJV) This quote from Thomas Jefferson is not in the Constitution, but he did make this quote because he was concerned that a state church would rein too much power in government, something the founders of our nation escaped from in Europe. Today this quote is used to promote the notion that Christians have no say-so in government, or be ostracized and excluded from influence in public schools. All of our founding fathers believed in a creator God and gave great credence to the Holy Scriptures. They certainly would be horrified to see how secularized we have become.

When it comes to understanding evolution and creation both should be presented as popular theories about life and neither should forced upon our children. Evolution requires a great leap of faith and it promotes survival of the strongest instead of real meaning and purpose in life. Creation theory gives our children hope and a sense of responsibility, and there is no lack of scientific evidence. But the most obvious and compelling evidence is to just observe the beauty and order of all creation.

On the basis of fairness young people deserve some representation on this issue, and because Christians pay taxes and support public education they deserve representative coursework in schools as an option; especially on the theories of life. "Faith is the substance of things hoped for, evidence of things not seen." (KJV)

CHAPTER 7

PLOTS AGAINST GOD

*O*bama's administration has from the beginning created policies that are attempting to steal away God given rights and freedoms. Obama's administration has also chosen to abandon Israel with unkind policies that favor the Palestinians. Truly, America has not fully woke up to all the attempts his administration is doing, but I am thankful for the Tea Party grass-root movement that was largely responsible for removing many House members with a more conservation core of politicians. But, we need to do more as a nation to renew our faith and trust in God. It is not enough to vote in politicians who only want to balance the budget and stop the excessive spending and immense debt. We must look to God to help us back to our Judeo-Christian roots.

The Bible gives us ample warning of nations who are swayed into believing that they will be protected and prosper by promoting a purely secular government. Consider the words of King David in Psalms chapter two.

"Why are the nations so angry? Why do they waste their time with futile plans? The kings of the earth prepare for battle; the rulers plot together against the Lord, and against his anointed one. Let us break their chains, they cry, and free ourselves from slavery to God. But the one who rules in heaven laughs. The Lord scoffs at them. Then in anger he rebukes them, terrifying them with his fierce fury. For the Lord declares, I have place my chosen king on the throne in Jerusalem, on my holy mountain." The king proclaims the Lord's decree: "The Lord said to me, "You are my son. Today I have become your Father. Only ask, and I will give you the nations as your inheritance, the whole earth as your possession. You will break them with an iron rod and smash them like clay pots." Now then, you kings, act wisely! Be warned, you rulers of the earth! Serve the Lord with reverent fear, and rejoice with trembling. Submit to God's royal Son, or he will become angry, and you will be destroyed in the midst of all your activities, for his anger flares up in an instant. But what joy for all who take refuge in him!" (Psalm 2)

Not only will a nation not prosper who choose not to honor his royal Son, but there is a real danger in being destroyed.

Understand Who God Is

The Quran is the Islamic holy book. It contains 114 chapter, or surahs, that govern religious, civil, commercial and military affairs. To the Muslims it has incalculable importance to them; as it directly affects social, cultural, educational, and religious value. It was codified into one test by Muhammad's followers shortly after his death. Muhammad could neither read nor write, and it is noteworthy that no translation is considered genuine Quran. It is believed by some that Muhammad experienced convulsions with visions and dreams and at a time later his words or sayings were put into a book called the "Hadith." Muhammad himself thought he was visited by demons during his experience, but his mother convinced him it was the voice of God. He did become a great military leader during and after the crusades, and he was quite ruthless. On one occasion he be-headed six hundred Jews who were living at peace with him.

It is noteworthy that there are more than a few distinct differences between Islam and Christianity, and important points about the nature of their god. God's name seems to be thrown around quite a bit these days especially when an atheist wants to put him in a bad light, but some serious observations and comparisons need to be made before we pass judgment on him. What kind of god is he? Is he always holy? Is he always good? Can he keep these divine attributes by also being a god of justice? Is he a god motivated by hate and revenge? Lets see, the Bible describes him as a God who is the "same yesterday, today, and forever," "with whom there is no variableness," (James 1:17). A God who loves us, who gave us His Son; (John 3:16). God commended his love towards us, while we were yet sinners," (Romans 5:8). A God who cannot lie; "In hope of eternal life, which God who cannot lie, promised before the world began," (Titus 1:2). A God who forgives and teaches forgiveness, not an "eye for an eye," no, rather turn the other cheek (Matthew 5:38-39). A God who offers salvation and eternal life, yes, "for by grace are you saved through faith and not of yourselves, it is the gift of God;" (Ephesians 2:8-9).

The Quran claims Allah is one God, who can change to suite his purposes; Surah 2:106. Allah hates sinners, "I will certainly fill hell with the Jinn (devils or demons) and men together;" (Surah 32:113). It is also alarming that the Quran advocates revenge upon Allah's perceived enemies, in order for a follower to keep his duty to Allah; Surah 2:194. I am of the persuasion that the more radical and sincerest followers of Islam are practicing their faith more literally than some of the Islamic followers who live in America who may be more peace loving. The primary issue here is the aggressive teachings of Islam whose goal is to dominate the world with its version of what is right and wrong. The fourth commandment of the Bible is "Thou shalt not kill." The truest intended meaning of this command means murder. My faith instructs me that I should live at peace with my neighbor for as much as it is possible, but my faith also instructs me to be subservient to authorities. If my government tells me I must go to war and kill, I will do so long as I determine it is for a just cause to stop murderers and to allow freedoms for people to live in equality with rights to believe in the true and living God. Our God does not have to intimidate or coerce people to believe, he has always allowed for freedoms of choice, and it is his will that all people be saved and come to know him, walk with him, and serve him willingly.

Islam is the largest of all religions, and its followers are aggressive in proselytizing its faith around the world. The growth rate in Europe, England, and even in the US and Canada is alarming. I believe it is a dangerous religion because of their radical Mullahs who teach their faith quite literally according to the teachings of Mohammed. It is a religion that once it dominates a land it will not tolerate other faiths or "isms" for that matter. This damming evidence has been demonstrated thousands of times by their atrocities in killing thousands of Christians and Jews, and peoples of different faiths or anyone they perceive as threats to them.

If what I have written thus far hasn't convinced you of the dangers of Islam, and you think I am blindly biased, I challenge you to read a book written by former Muslims. In the early 1980's, three brothers all serious devout Muslims and sons of a leader in the Islamic faith, surrendered their lives to the Lord Jesus Christ. They said, "It was God's gracious act towards them." There father disowned them, and they had to leave. According to Mohammad's sayings or "Hadiths," all three of his son's should have been executed for their change of heart. They did not see their father again until four days before his death, and he died a Muslim. Today Ergun and Emir Caner are Christian professors of church history and Theology, and authors of a very educational book titled "Unveling Islam."

A Prophet's Call for Repentance

Amos, a minor prophet spoke of Israel's disobedience and called for national repentance. In Amos chapter 5 he spoke unapologetically when he said "come back to the Lord and live." This warning was from God, although the nation did not heed his words and judgment soon followed. God will exalt any nation who promotes righteousness, but as the old Israel failed to remember God; our nation is following a similar path. I believe our nation has fallen from its former glory, and is in a desperate state of un-repentance. God's judgment will surely come to our nation if we do not humble ourselves and look to God.

Every American citizen must do self-examination, and allow God to renew their life, and then be impassioned to make responsible decisions in choosing the right kind of leaders who truly honor truth and justice and by following our great Constitution. Our great God did inspire our founding fathers in giving us this document of freedom. Our forefathers words were truly inspired by their Christian faith, and we would do well to remember their great sacrifice in their role in forming our government, and the blessings we have received since our founding.

Examine the words of Amos 5:4-15: This is what the Lord says to the house of Israel: "Seek me and live; do not seek Bethel, do not go to Gilgal, do not journey to Beersheba. For Gilgal will surely go into exile, and Bethel will be reduced to nothing. Seek the Lord and live, or he will sweep through the house of Joseph like a fire; it will devour, and Bethel will have no one to quench it. You who turn justice into bitterness and cast righteousness to the ground. He who makes the Pleiades and Orion, who turns blackness into dawn and darkens day into night, who calls for the waters of the sea and pours them out over the fence of the land. The Lord is his name. He flashes destruction on the stronghold and brings the fortified city to ruin, and you hate the one who reproves in court, and despise him who tells the truth. You trample on the poor and force him to give your grain. Therefore, though you have built stone mansions, you will not live in them; though you have planted lush vineyards, you will not drink their wine. For I know how many are your offenses and how great your sins. You oppress the righteous and take bribes and you deprive the poor of justice in the courts. Therefore the man keeps quiet in such times, for the times are evil. Seek good, not evil, that you may live. Then the Lord God Almighty will be with you, just as you say he is. Hate evil, love good;

maintain justice in the courts. Perhaps the Lord God Almighty will have mercy on the remnant of Joseph."

Even though Israel has disobeyed God many times in the past, he has not abandoned them to destruction and without hope. God did disperse the nation and scattered them to many nations of the world, and they have been cruelly treated throughout history. During the Spanish Inquisition alone nearly half a million Jews were murdered under the approval of the state church, and six million Jews were slaughtered in the holocaust of Nazi Germany, and many other unjust atrocities seem to follow them wherever they lived. Even Christians have chosen to hate them, but the irony of this is that Christianity would not come about without the Jew. The Bible was written by Jewish people, scribes, disciples, prophets, who were inspired to write truth by their God. Jesus Christ himself, a Jew, claimed to be the Son of God, Christians claim to be their savior and Lord. Yes, it is true that their national religion is Judaism, who clings to the Torah, the Old Testament books, rejecting the New Testament, therefore rejecting Christ as the Messiah. Still, today there is a growing number of Jewish Christians who accept Jesus Christ as the Messiah. And, I believe God is reserving a faithful remnant of his chosen, who have the faith of Abraham, from all over the world. But Israel is unique, the "apple of God's eye," God made a covenant with Abraham, saying; "I will make you a great nation; I will bless you and make your name great; and you will be a blessing. I will bless those who bless you, and I will curse him who curses you; and in you all the families of the earth shall be blessed Genesis 12:2-3."

Jeremiah spoke of a second exodus that would come in the future. The prophesy states: "Therefore behold, the days are coming," declares the Lord, "that it shall no more be said, "The Lord lives who brought up the children of Israel from the land of Egypt," but, The Lord lives who brought up the children of Israel from the land of the north and from all the lands where he had driven them. "For I will bring them back into their land which I gave to their fathers." (Jeremiah 16:14-15)

Today, Israel inhabits their own land, their own country where they can call home. Their government is strong, their military is among the finest in the world, and their economy is growing. Still, there are many who boycott Israeli goods, and many who plot their destruction, Israel's enemies seem to follow those who refuse to acknowledge the Judeo-Christian God, as the true and living God. God will remember those people and nations who do hateful things towards Israel. God's promise to Israel is simply understood in the last words of Amos. "I will plant Israel in their own land, never again to be uprooted from the land I have given them, says the Lord your God."

As Americans we need to understand God's unique relationship with Israel, that He will never abandon them. Our national policies with Israel are growing weaker, as radical Islamic factions are growing stronger, and even influencing us to abandon Israel because of weak leadership in the White House, who fail to see the big picture on whether God will bless and protect America. America's survival depends on a few but crucial factors. Individual and national repentance and how we treat Israel. God is waiting.

God's Promise To Israel

'Therefore say, "Thus says the Lord God: 'Although I have cast them far off among the Gentiles, and although I have scattered them among the countries, yet I shall be a little sanctuary for them in the countries where they have gone. Therefore say, "Thus says the Lord God: 'I will gather you from the peoples, assemble you from the countries where you have been scattered, and I will give you the land of Israel." And they will go there, and they will take away all its detestable thing and all its abominations from there. Then I will give them one heart, and I will put a new spirit within them, and take the stony heart out of their flesh, and give them a heart of flesh; (reconciliation), that they may walk in my statutes and keep my judgments and do them; and they shall be my people, and I will be their God; (reunion).

There are many passages in the Bible that give strong evidence that He (God) would bring the scattered Jewish peoples back to their homeland. The verse above is just one. Have you ever wondered how this tiny people group continues to survive and prosper when so many seek their destruction? All Arab nations are increasingly united in their growing hatred of Israel, attempting to justify their hatred from what they claim to be the inspired words of Allah. The whole world seems united in their support of the Palestinians instead of Israel. Abbas (Palestinian leader) recently made a statement that "Palestine" will be Jew free. That would include Jerusalem as its capitol, and that would mean that no Israeli would be allowed to live there. A Palestinian state means no Israeli presence. Clearly this is there goal, as Hama's terrorists who control the Gaza strip are stepping up their bombardment on Israeli communities with rockets. The Obama administrations are increasingly cowering to the UN, and the UN is united in their goal to eliminate the Jewish state. So, as the UN goes, the US will follow their lead towards the extermination of Israel, unless we as American citizens of God unite to replace misguided leaders in our nation who fail to see God's present and futuristic plan for Israel's protection and blessing to the world. Why should we ever consider going against God's promise to Israel? Why are we so bold in becoming so foolish? The answer to these questions rest with those who don't believe in God, and with those who don't respect or believe God's promise to Israel.

CHAPTER 8

PRESIDENT OBAMA

Presidents Obama & Trump Review

First, I think it is important to say that the American people have moved forward to overcome racial bigotry by voting for Mr. Obama, but I do not think many who voted for him were fully aware of his radical associations, and his real intentions to advance his ideological views and the lengths he would go to enhance the size of government through higher taxes. The major vehicles he used to promote his agenda was primarily government healthcare, EPA regulation, alternative energy, and global warming initiatives. He is very embolden to say things that are not true, and was seldom held accountable by a complicit liberal media who winked and nodded in approval. Even now the liberal media protect him as they did when he was in office, from any truthful criticism, and was usually dismissed with accusations of hatred and racism. President Obama promised civility with those who disagreed with him, but his promise to bring civility ring hallow as the opposite has occurred causing class warfare problems across the country during his two terms as President. Sadly, the seeds of unrest has now unleashed itself by the unruly protests from Black Lives Matter, Antifa, and other Marxist organizations. Up to that period of time I have never before seen an American President act or behave in such a radical manner as Mr. Obama. Never before have we seen a President on television as much as he, almost a daily occurrence. He seemed more intent on rallying his followers and his popularity so he can have his way in changing our form of government. Never before have we seen a President so beloved by NATO and radical leaders. He repeatedly expressed apologies for America as he continually does for supposed torture, for claiming we have occupied nations or forcing our form of government upon them. Accusing America of being uncaring, selfish and wasteful. Of course, our enemies cheer at such pronouncements. During his term he shut down European land based missile basis protecting bordering countries from Russia, and free countries were extremely concerned about his decision because at that time Russia invaded Georgia to occupy the oil pipeline that fed all of Europe. He thought he could negotiate with Iran's president Ahmoud Aminajab who promised to destroy Israel, who then and now are directly responsible for promoting and funding terrorism around the world. As well, Iran continues in its pursuit of nuclear weapons. This is of course left Israel in a precarious position, and what made it even worse is that he did not support Israel to be preemptive or to even protect itself from missile attacks.

Many foreign leaders and many in our own country have dreams of a global government, and Mr. Obama may even have hopes and dreams of being a world leader, and I believe there are some in powerful positions are pushing for this goal. If America should ever be stolen by the elites, loosing its sovereignty and its great Constitution, America will never again regain its freedom and liberty. If this should happen, America will be a part of a world government, with a one world banking system, and a one world currency. He and President Biden and nearly all democrats have successfully fooled enough people into thinking that America is always in a crisis, and believe me they are using the virus pandemic to promote more debt attempting to destroy our economic system of capitalism and then enact a new kind of government and control.

Obama's Slogan: "Hope and Change"

Writers for Obama have claimed 244 accomplishments, but have provided no documentation of results.

*Promised to improve federal agency transparency...no evidence

-Five policies were limitations on lobbyists...no study was found

-Promised to hold open meetings with Republican leaders...no study was found

-Claimed credit for phasing out the F-22 fighter plane...controversial

-Said he would close Guantanamo Bay detention facility and bring terrorists to trial...did not happen

-Cancelled anti-ballistic program with Poland and Czechoslovakia from Russia...he did

-Fulfilled promise to remove all American troops from Iraq by Aug. 2010...4 years later Islamic State groups had retaken major portions of Iraq and Syria.

-Authorized SEALS to recapture maritime captain taken hostage by Somali pirates...? About leadership

-Sent envoy to Myanmar to obtain release of American hostage...no results

-Hosted nuclear non-proliferation talks...no comment made

-Authorized 789 billion economic stimulus program, coordinated with George W. Bush...executed

President Obama served two terms yet his accomplishments paled in comparison to President Trump who only served one term. Obama failed to even help poorer Americans of all colors, and people noticed his lack of doing anything notably helpful to ease life for the poorer class. This may have led to poorer people to vote for Trump in the next election. African Americans were concerned that illegal immigrants were taking away job opportunities and rightfully so, and so many in turn voted for Trump who did a lot to shut the border down. The percentage of African American voters rose significantly for Trump and Republicans because they promised to do something on the border, while democrats were chiming about amnesty and open borders. The ideological views of Obama caused concern for Cuban Americans especially in Florida because they experienced the extreme hardships of communist Cuba, so many chose to vote for Trump instead of Clinton in the next election.

Now we see under President Biden's administration we see complete open borders. I believe it is time for Americans who are on the fence on how to vote. Better think long and hard before voting for democrats who are intent on radical policies. Whether it be open borders with all the associated problems of drugs and gangs, diseases, no virus vaccines, free government money, possible terrorists coming into the country, and of course more votes for the democrat party to rule our nation. The Marxists who control much of the democrat party may be biting off more than they can handle because the American people are slowly noticing how things have gone to hell so to speak since Biden took office. From outrageous stimulus trillion dollar packages which will result in higher taxes, and inflation through the roof, higher fuel costs for vehicles and home, and the ever explosive school boards trying to impose "critical race theory" upon our kids. Judge Merrick Garland attempting to arm the FBI to arrest peaceful protestors. Mask mandates for students even playing sports, and now working on mandating vaccine shots for younger children in all public schools will cause an immense uproar. Now we have already seen corporations and large businesses forcing employees to get shots or lose their job, even thousands of nurses are being forced into vaccine mandates no matter their health issues or religious beliefs. Parents are upset with libraries allowing children to be exposed to pornography books and explicit literature and pictures.

Everything is getting higher in costs, and the problems of availability of products has become an increasing problem. Christmas may never be the same.

All of these things and more are invading our country and President Biden is just getting started. These democrat policies are not reasonable and are meant to cripple us into government submission. Do not go along just to get along. Please remember at voting time to free ourselves from Marxist policies, and whatever you do not vote democrat, and do not vote for fake republicans.

President Trump's Slogan: "Make America Great Again"

President Trump served one term and rallied his followers by campaigning all over the country. Many Americans loved his slogan, and he vowed that America will never become a socialist country. Liberal media and his enemies sneered at his pronouncements at every opportunity. His slogan implied that the greatness of America had diminished especially during Obama's terms as President. Mr. Trump rubbed some people wrong with his open brashness, and was looked upon by some as arrogance. The democrat media like CNN, MSNBC and CBS reported extreme bias against Mr. Trump and expressed a constant drumbeat of attacks on Russian collusion, accusing him a number of unproven claims. Mr. Trump called-out these media outlets at rally's as "fake news." The opposing media and even Fox news would find opportunity to criticize him, especially when he called-out Republican "Rhino's," who claimed to support conservative values and love for America, but more often than not supported democrat policies. There was no middle ground for support of President Trump, either people loved him, or they hated him. Even when his policies were good for America, some people could not distinguish between supported him or rejecting him., and people often become offended by his confident speech or his personality, and regrettably did not hear the truth of his words, and the wisdom of his policies. I believe it is fair to say that President Trump built a prosperous economy. Under his leadership America gained 7 million jobs, middle-class families income increased nearly by six-thousand. Unemployment decreased to 3.5%, jobless claims hit nearly a 50 year low as unemployment insurance hit lowest on record.

Poverty rates for African American's and Hispanic's American's reached record lows, and lifted 7 million off of food stamps. Wages for everybody with low income and blue collar workers was a 16% pay increase. Trump brought jobs, factories, and industries back to the USA. He also initiated innovative new technologies to the market in farming and agriculture. Trump signed the tax cut and Jobs Act, the largest reform package in histo ry. Most notably Trump cut business tax rate from 35% down to 21%. Even though this is only a brief review it should not be overlooked. From his massive deregulation for businesses and workers which resulted in more money for the American people.

President Trump...cont.

He also promoted fair and reciprocal trade by withdrawing from the Trans-Pacific Partnership (TPP), ended (NAFTA) and created new protections for American manufacturers (auto-farmers-dairy) and workers potentially creating over a half-million new jobs. He took action to stop the outsourcing of American jobs overseas. He negotiated with Japan to slash tariffs and opened a farmers market, and with South Korea he re-negotiated a free trade agreement. With China Trump negotiated 200 billion worth of exports and opened over 4,000 American facilities to exports while tariffs remained in effect. He imporsed actions to confront unfair trade practices and put Americans first, and yes he did impose tariffs on hundreds of billions worth of Chinese goods.

He directed efforts to halt and punish the Chinese government from profiting from American innovation and intellectual property. Trade with numerous countries vastly improved. Trump promoted American Energy Independence initiative and unleashed America's oil and natural gas potential. He prevented Russia energy coersion across Europe and stopped there pipeline.

Although President Trump was highly critisized for his handling of the virus pandemic by his enemies, he did suspend travel from China and saved thousands of lives by his actions. He imposed travel restrictions and warned citizens to avoid international travel. He created a task force to combat the virus, and called on the United Nations for holding China more accountable for their handling of the virus by allowing the virus to spread around the world, and their denial that the virus was created at the Wuhan Lab and escaped somehow by mishandling, or possibly intentially released as a biological weapon by the Chinese military leaders. One thing is for sure overwhelming number of doctors agree that this virus did not come from nature, and had to have been created by human intervention.

President Trump launched "Operation Warp Speed" to produce vaccines in just nine months; five times faster that any vaccine developed in American history. Pfizer and Moderna's vaccines have proven to effective at approximately 95%, and shortly after the Johnson & Johnson vaccine arrived.

As we now know these vaccines are not effective for a lifetime and booster shots may be required. As people are contracting the virus even though they have had their shots, but the recovery rate seems to be better, but their is still conjecture on what is true or not true. We are still learning about the virus, but President Trump was successful in getting the vaccines out quickly to the American people.

Facts about President Trump:

-nominated and confirmed 230 federal judges, and appointed (3) supreme judges

-a climate change skeptic: halted the Paris Climate Accord (unknowable amount of$ saved!)

-pledged 10 million jobs, 1 million new small businesses, income tax cuts, tax credits for businesses

-does not see racism a systematic problem

-supported the "right to bear arms," and tightening on background checks

-initiated the building of the southern wall to Mexico, and stopping illegal immigrants entering illegally

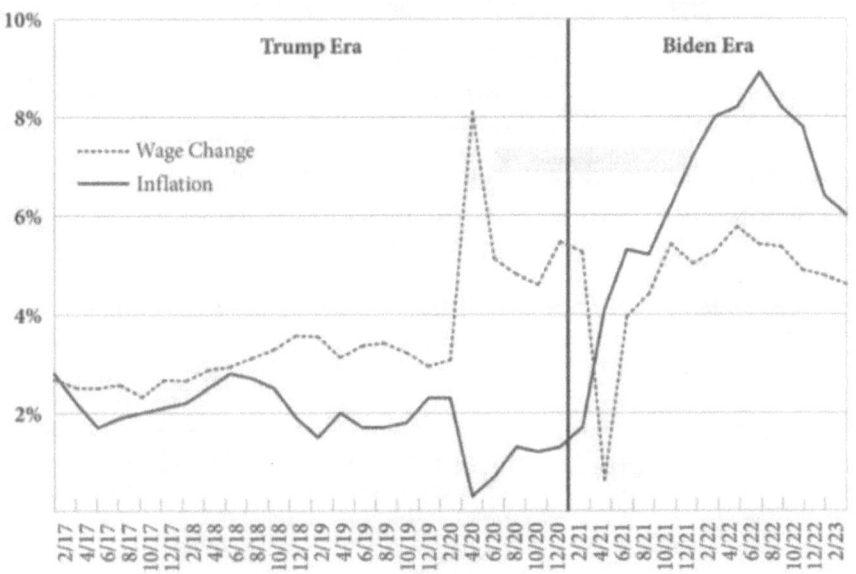

Article in 'Biden Economy and How it can be fixed' – Volume 52, Number 3 – March 2023, Andrew F. Puzder

The negative impact on American workers has been tremendous. The chart above traces wages (or income) versus inflation as reflected in the Consumer Price Index. The dotted line is wage growth and the solid line is inflation. The big surge where the dotted line jumps way up reflects the federal spending during the pandemic. To the left of that jump, we see that during the Trump administration, wages were up about three percent and inflation about two percent. To the right on the chart, we see what happened after Biden took office. Within a couple of months, inflation shoots way up above wages-indeed, the month inflation crossed over wages was March 2021, the very month Congress passed The American Rescue Plan.

But there's even more bad news. Since so many people are not working and wages have been declining for those who are working due to inflation, savings have now declined to historic lows-in fact, to the lowest level we've seen going back to 1959. People are running out of cash, and as a result they are using credit cards. Credit card debt when Biden took office was at $748 billion and it stayed there until May 2021-again, until shortly after the passage of The American Rescue Plan-at which point it began to shoot way up to what is now $986 billion, the highest level of credit card debt in our history. And this is happening at a time when the Federal Reserve is compelled to continue raising interest rates to try to battle inflation.

Excess demand and low supply: This was the situation when Biden took office in 2021. And as any student of elementary economic knows, when demand exceeds supply you get inflation. Isn't it pretty obvious what should be done in that situation? You should adopt policies that juice supply and avoid adopting policies that juice demand. Instead, the Biden Administration proceeded to do the exact opposite.

President Joe Biden:

President Biden pushed through more executive orders in his first few months in office than any other president. Now president Biden through executive older is hiring another 87,000 IRS agent doubling the size of the government agency. A question that needs to be asked is why? Some suggest it is a governmental money grab, and to create more fear and harassment for the American people. Even more concerning to our freedom is the thought that a party is influencing the IRS for political reasons. We need to always remember that the IRS agency are government employees who are elected by the people and it is quite possible that they could be influenced by a political party to their bidding. Giving government even more power and control over our people.

The democrat leadership are embolden to push forward their radical agenda, and this is their window of opportunity with a complicent President. The southern border is open and a complete mess as thousands pour into this country illegally, and President Biden winks and nods in approval, or lies to the american public that the border is secure. He supports radical climate change and says stupid things like the greatest threat to America is Global warming. He says things like this to promote the "new green deal." He also promotes free education and medicare for all who have not paid anything. If you took all the money from the rich it would not touch this kind of massive spending.

Joe Biden's running mate was declared to be ComIara Harris. This selection is curious because in the debates she was extremely critical of him on his issues with touching women and racist issues from his past. I believe the democratic leadership is totally behind this decision for two reasons. The first reason, they want her to be Joe's replacement because they know his mental health is at doubt for him to finish his term. Second, Harris is considered by many in the legislature to be the most radical selection for vice-president., and will be used to promote Marxist/socialist policies. She comes across as charming, but believe me her policies will not be charming or american. Things like open borders, guns will be taken away, our Constitution will be done away with, radical judges will be appointed, taxes will go much higher, and this is just a small list. It can be summed up by saying every freedom we enjoy and believe in today will be in danger. Big government will grow and our freedoms will diminish! The democrats have gone to great lengths to destroy President Trump, even now after he left office.

The liberal media have no shame that constantly ignore any truthful news and disguise their narrative story reporting which is nothing more than opinion news. All we heard from them for over two years was the Russian hoax, proven to be totally false, and no they have not apologized to the american people. The media promoted the impeachment hoax, slamming former President Trump over the origins of covid 19, and even stealing credit from him for advancing the vaccine. Giving credit to President Biden and Doctor Fauchi instead, who deserve no credit. Then you got Nancy Pelosi advancing another false narrative or lie if you prefer that the riot at the White House by Trump supporters was an armed ressurection. Not one gun was recovered or found! Conclusion, we the American people need to punish these radical media outlets by not watching or supporting them or their networks, or businesses they are associated with, because we must diminish their influence on the American public. This is a pivotal moment in America, the stakes are high, and we must fight back if we want to advance our policies to insure that freedom in America is protected.

State of Affairs/Political & Culture War

I am curious to know what our founding fathers would think of America's moral decline. Even though there is great advancement in technology, infrastructure and highways, vehicles, computers, and all the conveniences of life nowadays, would certainly amaze them to see all the advances. But I believe they would be horrified to see how we have declined. To see how the family structure is being re-defined and traditional marriages are being abandoned in favor of a "woke" culture value system. To see so many abandoned churches, public education preventing God and the bible to be a moral guide to our children. Our public education system has chosen an economical values system over and above a moral values system, and it shouldn't surprise us to see crime rising in our nation. We shouldn't be shocked to see the chaos and the unruly disrespect for authority starting with God and the Ten commandments, our nations president, law enforcement, and to parents. Very little love for our neighbors has been replaced with self-love or narcissism. How can a nation get back to its roots to love God instead of money? The Bible says that the "love of money is at the root of all kinds of evil." If we put away our excessive love affair with money, and put God back to His rightful place in our government and educational systems, and in our culture, and in our lives, God will bless us again. Love and truth must go hand in hand by God's people and for them to live out their faith not by word only, but by a living example.

Since 2012, when I first wrote my book about my concerns of what President Obama was promoting was in fact racial disharmony and promotion of a Marxist/Socialist revolution. I tried to make the case that what he did was unprecedented, creating racial division among the American people, disguised as "social justice," and now promoted as "white privilege." The seeds of discord that he planted is becoming more and more plain to see in the riots being promoted all over our nation. Especially where democratic mayors and governors allowing insurrection and unruly behavior in cities burning and destroying businesses, stealing, and actually hurting and killing police who were told not to arrest the rioters.

The liberal or democratic media outlets are controlled by democratic leadership and they are working in harmony to change our form of government, and they are fervently working together to destroy Donald J. Trump. There was a time when media outlets valued truth in their reporting no matter what their political bias; but no longer. Now they callously speak slanderous lies about a president or anyone who challenges their viewpoints. Truth is truth, no matter where the story leads, and it should have no bias towards one party or the other! Today there is no shame in media reporting, no accountability to report the news. They rely on people's emotions who half-heartedly pay attention, who are swayed by political opinion and not truthful news reporting. The left-wing media outlets pick and choose stories that fit their narrative. This is especially true concerning police and law enforcement. Police violence is rare in our country, but it has occurred. Police authority is often challenged, and sometimes are attacked or even shot. Is it not reasonable for them to react to the violence that is being perpetrated upon them? I will agree that there needs to be better screening of candidates who want to be police officers. Not all are wired with the appropriate patience and judgement needed, and maby some policy changes need to be made. The American people need to see a reliable chart of police violence that is substantiated because it is extremely rare. But one thing is for sure, we cannot survive as a nation without laws and those who enforce the laws! Law abiding citizens are becoming more and more concerned, buying guns for protection, more people are leaving the big cities, and I don't blame them.

"Racism" is the calling card that will lead to war. Our nation experienced this already in the war between the states, and this fact shouts loudly to us this truth-sadly, that only war will stop this evil. Abraham Lincoln spoke to us this truth, "that a nation divided against itself cannot stand!" This is exactly why President Lincoln chose to engage the war, and that was to preserve the union and our nation as it was founded. "One nation under God." If we want to preserve our nation again as it was founded, we must be very active against the radicals who kill and intimidate those of us who want to live in peace. And, quite frankly we must not bow our knees to appease on any level! Professional sports owners who allow athletes to bow to their knees while the national anthem is being played is repulsive. And to remove our national anthem is wrong! Loyal viewers are being lost on sports channels, and I have heard from many friends that they will not watch any sports if they continue disrespecting our flag and our nation. Protests should not be allowed or be used as an opportunity on a national stage for political, or for any reason. Fans just want to watch competitive sports period! Presidents of these large sport organizations need to be censored until they understand that there is an appropriate time and place to make a protest, and it's not in the sports arena. Believe me, if we can affect their pocket-book they will stop their nonsense.

What is the correlation of what a bad cop did to a black man have to do with being ashamed of our flag or nation? What is the correlation or reasoning behind destroying our monuments? Why are supposed

"Black Lives Matter" crowds labelled as peaceful when they are c[early not peaceful? Infiltrated by people who openly admit they are Marxists and want to overrule' our government. Why is the left-wing media reporting a false narrative that all these protests are peaceful, or give accurate reporting on what is really going on? Why do mayors and governors of large cities want to de-fund the police? The answer to these questions is, Marxist revolution! We need to remember the democratic leadership of today led by Pelosi and Shumer, and of course by President Biden are pushing for and allowing radical elements and politicians and judges to rule us with an iron fist. President Biden seems open to radical change when he supports "defunding the police," open borders, radical "climate change" policies, universal healthcare, and the wish list goes on and on. All of this goes back to President Obama" s quote and desire to fundamentally change America. Destroying all semblance of history, or anything that would make us proud of our nation. Public education has largely been taken over by a radical element in the teachers union not to teach American history. America we need the older generation to help our younger generation to help them understand what is going on in schools. Because our youth are being indoctrinated to believe in Marxist ideas of governance. If we do not stop the radicals who have infiltrated our government from city to state, to our federal government and our public education we will eventually loose our nation. Because the older generation will soon pass away and the younger generation will rule our nation. We must do all we can to help them understand the importance of factual history, whether it shines a light on the good or the bad-we can all benefit from its truth, if its taught in truth, and not by revisionist historians who want to cloud the real story! A famous quote by Edmond Burke, bears repeating; "if we don't learn from the mistakes of the past, we are doomed to repeat it." This is why it is important to teach American history to our kids, and it wouldn't hurt for the older generation to brush up on what they forgot. As I mentioned in the forward of my book, a great historian David Barton would be a good start or refresher for anyone to read. As well, read other respected historians.

"Black Lives Matter" leaders openly proclaim that they are Marxists, and have been trained to teach others this kind of belief system. Antifa has its roots in Russia, and it has a long history that resided in West Germany, moved to England, and eventually invaded the United States. During the city riots the peaceful protestors did not know all that was planned by these radical groups, who are being funded. Sadly, peaceful protestors were overwhelmed by the Marxists, and some gang elements joined in the fray to loot and shoot people because they knew that the police were restricted from doing anything to stop them. I also predict that the White House riots were motivated by the Marxists who pre-planned the whole incident. Possibly in time the real truth will come to light.

A question that seriously needs to be asked is, who is funding these radical groups, and who are some these people who are destroying monuments of Christopher Columbus, founding fathers, civil war heroes, and even presidents like George Washington and Abraham Lincoln? I mentioned in the beginnings of my book, that there are organizational forces who are behind a socialist/Marxist movement. I believe 'George Soros' is a prime candidate because he has a history of nation building for socialism and a one world government or global governance. I am sure that there are others who are behind this movement in our government, large corporations, social media, and international influences. So, how can we prove to the American people this truth. We have seen the relentless attacks upon our former president from liberal media and social media. From Russia collusions to instigating a supportive crowd to attack the White House. Their unfounded attacks go on day after day because they are afraid of his influence, and possibly running for office again. Any president that espouses freedom that comes from God, and not big government will be attacked by democrat media, social media, democrat politicians, public education, and radical groups espousing Marxism like Black Lives Matter and Antifa. A good president will protect our country from radical elements who are promoting sedition and treason. If we are to survive as a nation we must support and pray for presidents and leaders, for the Lord himself to grant them wisdom. No president can fight this battle alone. This is a battle for all freedom loving Americans, and we must unite for the cause of freedom. All people have suffered from the covid virus pandemic, and obviously God has allowed it to happen. Why? I cannot say with certainty but possibly He wants your attention, and whether you know it or not, we need Him. Not all people have forgotten God, but far too many people live their lives without any worship or acknowledgement of God. Friends, we need Him in our lives!

Referring back to those who are destroying monuments of great people of the past. Many of these people are teachers in public education, who are in support of radical groups and socialism. Some are college students who are not focused on working, but rather are focused on destroying history.

Curiously, they are nearly all white people. I think any President needs to crack down on these people, and college professors who are the religious leaders to speak, and real promoters of Marxism/socialism. Presidents of these liberal colleges also need to answer to the public and be open as to why they constantly hire liberal teachers and professors. Our tax dollars are supporting these public institution, but they are not teaching on a balanced approach. They teach leftist ideology, and a total disrespect for God, and our nation's history. They do not speak for all people, and since we help support them with our taxes, they need to be held to account to represent our values as much as anybody else.

Dr. Anthony Fauci/Covid 19 Origins & Lockdowns

Doctor Fauci is among the highest paid government employee that we the public support. He hold immense influence and responsibility to keep Americans safe amid a pandemic. But, has he done a good job in advising us about the truth? Has he provided leadership and a good plan to keep Americans safe? Dr. Fauci has given us shifting advice on masks on numerous occasions, and shifting advice on lockdowns as well. Dr. Fauci, the NIH and WHO organizations have done a great disservice by downplaying existing drugs that can now, and could have saved people's lives from the virus. Over a thousand doctors have shouted from the rooftops that existing drugs like ivermectin and hydroxychloriqin, and other drugs are safe and effective, that can save people from dying. Dr. Kory supported by republican Senator Ron Johnson, claimed that 62% of less deaths could have occurred with early treatment of the above mentioned proven drugs. Dr. Kory said that as many as a hundred thousand lives or more in this country alone could have been saved!

Why did Dr. Fauci and his cohorts who support him suppress this information to the American public? Why did big tech (you tube, twitter, facebook), censor these doctors from relaying this information to the public? Why did democrat supported media downplay and discredit these safe and proven drugs? Certainly a lot of questions need to be answered by Dr. Fauci and the CDC. Billions of dollars were given to these vaccine companies to produce a vaccine quickly. But, because it was done so quickly, they did not anticipate the long range results and protection from getting the virus again even after being vaccinated. Doctors admit that the covid 19 vaccines were not designed like a polio vaccine to last a lifetime. This is not to say that the vaccines do not help, it depends largely upon one's immune system and health, and of course one's age has a lot to do with a person's recovery if infected by the virus.

Did Dr. Fauci involve himself in politics when he discredited former President Trump? Were there massive money making schemes or kickbacks for the democrat party? One thing for sure is that far less money would have been spent by using the older, yet proven effective drugs with early treatment, and far many more lives would have been saved.

In my humble opinion, Dr. Fauci is no hero to the American people, and now they discover his e-mails which is disturbing in itself by his providing funding to the Wuhan lab, that quite possibly manufactured this horrible virus. And, really no-one really knows if the Chinese government (Communist) intentionally released it upon the world, or if it happened by accident. The virus is so complicated that many officials agree that it had to have been created by human intervention, and not created by nature. Former President Trump is gradually being vindicated for his claim that the virus came from the Wuhan lab. Investigation of Dr. Fauci is on-going and it should be because American's deserve to know the truth.

The Necessary Purge:

A righteous purge needs to occur in our nation, not only in government, but also in all American people, and especially in God's chosen faithful. In Chronicle 7:14, it states "If my people, who are called by my name, will humble themselves and pray and seek my face and turn from their wicked ways, then I will hear from heaven and will forgive their sin and will heal their land." In Psalm 19:9-11 it states "The fear of the Lord is pure, enduring forever. The ordinances of the Lord are sure and altogether righteous, they are more precious than gold. By them is your servant warned; in keeping them is great reward."

There is no doubt that God's laws and ordinances are not respected in today's society, and although we have always lived in an imperfect world, God did not make it this way. Since our rebellion and disobedience to God in the beginning, God has never abandoned us without hope. His grace and mercy is waiting for our change of heart. This has already been proven by multitude thousands who have experienced His forgiveness and blessing, and the examples he gave us to encourage us, and instruct us in His great inspired book, the Bible. So, we really do not have an excuse to ignore it, as we have done for too long. His Holy Spirit calls out to all of us. Will we hear his call and respond to Him in these troubled days we are all experiencing?

The "purge" from the radical left is directed against all "constitutional conservatives" and Christians. But, the real purge should be in the reverse against all activist movements from the "far left." It has been a long trek for the Marxists, but they have been effective. They have successfully infiltrated the media as far back as Carl Marx. The public education union controls the curriculum who are in fact indoctrinating our kids into Marxism ideas of thought, and a re-writing of our American history. Activist politicians and judges seem to abound in our society. Social media is now on board with the radical media outlets who are subverting our voice. Corporations seem to be okay with socialist and Marxist ideas of governance with over taxation, and monopolies over small businesses. Government agencies cannot be trusted anymore who have not been elected by the people, so they can become corrupted by powerful political party influence. For example, agencies such as the FBI, CIA, and even the CDC. All of these powerful agencies have conspired against former President Trump. As Christians, we should pray for our leaders and vote responsibly as we should all do, but if our leaders refuse God's leading and forgiveness there evil way's will not be purged, then it becomes obvious that the people they serve will suffer!

A few suggestions that came to mind I would like to share with you, and I am sure there are many more ideas from very intelligent people who love freedom. #1. I think we should enact policies to impose term limits, if we should ever gain power again. As well enact policies that would prevent judicial activism, or re-writing Constitutional laws. #2. Eliminate protections to social media/tech giants like google, twitter, facebook who are silencing conservative speech which they do not agree with, or any speech for that matter. #3. Enact policies to prevent any known socialist or Marxist communist from running or who is currently in office to serve in public office. On grounds that it is a danger to our existing government and Constitution. I believe these radical ideas of governance promote sedition and treason. #4. Support all bordering states that are being invaded by illegal aliens, encouraged to come into our country illegally by our President. Since this executive order is illegal and unconstitutional any Governor has a duty and a right to secure the border with or without a judge, or federal authority approval. Replace all border agents if necessary, with the National Guard until the border is secure. This would create a face-off between federal government and state government, but I believe it is necessary especially in Texas. Anyone can enter now, no vaccinations for covid, no vaccinations for any disease, TB is very common. Thousands upon thousands are entering our country and moved especially in states that lean Republican. A clever and insidious plan for Democrates to win elections. Any President or any state governor has a duty to protect its people, and to protect a free democracy from invasion period!

Imagining Freedom:

Imagining freedom in America seems to be more of a dream than a reality, but then again, if you don't hope for positive change and plant the seeds for a better future, hope will always be deferred or disappointed. Our founding fathers planted the seeds of freedom, but in todays world many Americans and government officials have forgotten and diminished the values of freedom. Our founders were dreamers but they were more than that because they put their dreams into action, and even though their situation was even more dire than what we face today, they did not give up but continued their fight for freedom. And, because of their stedfast sacrafice, America became the most free nation that this world has ever seen. I dream for a free America as intended by our founders, simply put, free from big government. The Declaration of Independence makes it clear that we should 'dissolve the political bands when they attempt to assume powers over 'natures God, who attempt to steal away unalienable rights of life, liberty and the ability to own property. Those who endanger our rights of freedom of religion, freedom of speech, and a free press, then we are instructed that 'whenevever any form of government becomes destructive of these ends, it is the right of the people to alter or to abolish it and to institute new government."

The first and most basic responsibility we have as Americans to God and country is to pray and walk with 'natures God' everyday, and to responsibly provide care to one's family. The second most basic responsibility is to vote responsibly! It would benefit us greatly if we simply placed our faith in God, to believe in America as it was founded, and to always be cautious of trusting media sources or any one political party.

Education

Young adults are attracted to socialism because they think in the immediate like free education and free other stuff. If all people understood the history and failures of socialism, they would not be so quick to trust in this kind of governance. Any responsible President has a basic duty to protect our country. This includes protecting us from foreign influences to change our for form of government. A President needs to investigate all powerful people or organizations who are promoting the funding of radical groups, and this includes politicians in their own party, media, and education. Federal funding for public education needs to be scrutinized until they teach a more balanced approach of liberal, moderate, and conservative viewpoints. American history must be a requirement and Constitutional teachings as intended by our founders. This requirement of American history and insuring teaching an honest view of our founders visions and accomplishments. This is crucial to our children's education, as well as the basics of math, english and science. This balanced requirement is needed for our children's education in all public schools and colleges. Any school that refuses to teach education in a balanced manner must not receive one dime from federal government. If radical colleges with their 'one point of view' want to exist they must support themselves; but really I would rather not exist at all, because they have proven to be indoctrination house of socialism. Colleges are getting out of control in not allowing conservative speakers or teachers for that matter, out of control costs which is mostly channeled to college presidents and professors. Sedition alone is grounds to investigate these public institutions.

What we need is a ground swell of support for private schools and home schooling, until our grade and high schools get back to teaching from books that have not been infiltrated with socialist leanings and a diminishing of true american history.

If we are to survive as nation under God, we must attack the liberal strongpoints in education because our young people are our most valued treasure for the future. The 'teachers union' must be abolished or re-done entirely'! There is no doubt the teachers union has become too powerful and controlled by the wrong people. We need to insure that better teachers are hired who love our country and reject teachers who are intent on indoctrinating our kids by enforcing a corrupt curriculum. A disturbing curriculum currently being advanced is 'critical race theory' which teaches that all white people are inherently racists. Who in their right mind would teach such nonsense? Thankfully there is a push back as parents are questioning school boards reasoning and push for 'critical race theory' to be taught to our kids. Thank God!

Failed Policies of the Past

President Obama has told us that we need to break away from the "failed policies of the past", but history tells another story of governmental policies that failed not unlike what he is leading us into. National Socialism has a profound history of failure. But the kind of policies and beliefs our founding fathers gave us advances the prospect of success. We need to only remember the great words given to us in the Declaration of Independence, "We find these truths to be self-evident, that all men are created equal, endowed by their Creator with certain inalienable rights of life, liberty, and pursuit of happiness (property).

Socialists in Government

It is reported that there are eighty-one socialists in Congress. At one time they called themselves the Democratic Socialists of America. Now they prefer to be called the Congressional Progressive Caucus. Obviously they are afraid of being labeled "socialists" or "communists", so they have branded themselves "progressives", knowing full well that people react more positively to the "progressive" title. What needs to be clearly understood by citizens is that there is no change in ideology just because of a name change. The Congressional Progressive Caucus or (CPC) is fully committed to neo-Marxist ideology. They are also closely tied in with the Socialist International group or (SI). The goal of CPC is to centralize government to gain more power over the will of the American people. "Social Justice" is their by-word which promotes the re-distribution of wealth. They intend to fleece corporations and the wealthy with higher taxes, and increase social programs that ultimately steal our freedoms. The CPC was established in 1991 by six members of the United States House of Representatives. They are; Bernie Sanders (I-VT), Rob Dellums (D-CA), Lane Evans (D-IL), Thomas Andrews (D-ME), Peter DeFazio (D-OR) and Maxine Waters (D-CA).

In 2005 the Progressive Caucus organized a document which adheres to the following positions;

Establish universal, government provided healthcare

Trade agreements that favor the rights of foreign workers over Americans

The right of all workers to organize into labor unions and engage in collective bargaining

The abolition of USA Patriot Act

The legalization of same sex marriage

A complete pullout from the wars in Iraq and Afganistan

An increase in income tax rate

An increase in welfare spending by the federal government

Advocates of One World Government

Quotes:

"To stabilize and regulate a truly global economy, we need some global system of political decision making. In short, we need a global society to support our global economy."

George Soros
Socialist Billionaire

"Some even believe we are part of a secret cabal working against the best interests of the United States characterizing my family and me as…conspiring with others around the world to build a more integrated global political and economic structure—one world if you will. If that's the charge, I stand guilty and I am proud of it."

David Rockefeller
Memoire

Conclusion

As I reminisce why I wrote this book I want people to take a hard look at the times we live in. Events are not normal, although an argument could be made that man has not been normal as God intended since his fall in the Garden of Eden. Still, it is unnerving to see all the upheaval around the world, and now we see a lot of social unrest in America. America is in a culture war, and it's like individual nations within a nation. Not everybody loves our flag or our nation, not everybody uses the English language, and certainly a lot of people are divided on the military efforts around the world. I think it can be accurately said, we are in a war of ideology, and the previous Obama administration and current administration are promoting it. A lot of people just don't want to accept the idea of a conspiracy coming from our highest elected official, and I agree it is difficult to believe. But, if one will take the time to investigate the policies Obama has enacted, and promoting, and as well examine the inconsistency of his words, I think you will at least agree with the words of Abraham Lincoln. Lincoln said, "A house divided against itself cannot stand". If we are to survive as a nation under God we must reach our children. Our youth are searching for meaning in life, and if they are not taught at an early age to know our nations great beginning, to know and respect the great morality code taught in the scriptures and most importantly to know the Christ who can set them free. Then, I fear our nation will be lost as we know it. But I believe in the greatness of America and its people, and I hope for God's patience and love to help us back to our roots. There must be a revival, but before that can happen there must be repentance and humility. How much that involves, only God knows.

In evaluating the times we live in consider the worlds intensifying hate against the nation Israel, and the world's economic struggles. Even as I write this, the European nations are collapsing economically. England is contemplating leaving the European coalition because of bailouts to Greece. Many other European nations are at the brink of collapse. Evidence is mounting that we are in the birth pangs of a "coming day", as the Bible puts it, "a day of Jacobs's trouble". Some think that if God is coming soon there is nothing we can do to change the course of our future. But if that were true then why did our great founders start the revolution? Why didn't we just accept the inevitable that England's overlords would defeat us, that we had no chance to win against the world's greatest military power of that period. The reason is that some dared to believe that God was with them and thus acted to preserve freedom. Only a third of our nations people were fully behind the revolution, but the cause was righteous, and I believe that God was their protector and with a mighty hand delivered our nation. Some may ask, why did God choose to help us become a nation? I think the answer can be found in Acts 1:8, when God gave the great mandate, "go into the world and preach the gospel"! I believe God uses people in any nation who are willing to propagate his truth and his purposes to reach lost people, and I believe he stays his judgment based upon our willingness to follow his commands. When God gave Moses the Ten Commandments a perfect standard to live by, he knew his followers would fail to keep it perfectly. The law is like a target at a hundred yards away and you're shooting at it with bow and arrow a thousand times a day all the days of your life. It would be impossible to hit the bull's eye every time. But the commandments were given to show the people their need for God, that only his mercy and grace could save them. But the commandments were given for us to strive for as a righteous standard. It is God's hope (I believe) that man would recognize just how utterly helpless he is without his dependence on God. The forefather of all true believers is Abraham. When God tested Abraham to sacrifice his only son, he obeyed God and came within a second of doing the act, when an angel stopped his hand. Was Abraham justified by works? "No, not before God, the Scriptures say that he believed God, and it was credited to him as righteousness." Romans 4:3. This great story is all centered upon trusting in the only one who can save us, and this trust is called faith. The best verse that comes to mind that explains this principle that leads to a right relationship with God is found in Ephesians 2:8,9, "for by grace are you saved, through faith, and this not from yourselves, it is the gift of God, not by works, so that no one can boast". God has provided us a perfect sacrificial lamb that was sacrificed on our behalf so that our sins can be forgiven, and be freed from the curse of the law. You see, the law of God only condemns us; it does not give us righteousness. God's perfect son frees us from our fallen nature and replaces it with a divine nature, thus he will instill in us the desire to share his truth and good news to the world.

We should do all we can to live in peace with our neighbors. This I believe is what God wants us to do, and his blessing will follow. For the scriptures say, "If you want a happy life and good days, keep your tongue from speaking evil, and keep your lips from telling lies. Turn away from evil and do good. Work hard at living in peace with others. The eyes of the Lord watch over those who do right, and his ears are open to their prayers. But the Lord turns his face against those who do evil", (1 Peter 3:10-12).

CHAPTER 9

A GLANCE AT OUR FIRST PRESIDENTS

George Washington

Short Biography: George Washington was born on February 22, 1732 in Virginia. He was an Episcopalian by religion. In 1759, Washington wedded Martha Dandridge Custis. In 1775, George Washington was the Commander-in-chief of the American Revolutionary Forces. He is the only President to be elected unanimously. He was not a member of any political party. On April 30, 1789, George Washington took his oath of office as the first President of the United States. Washington was one of two Presidents who signed the U.S. Constitution. He served one term as President, and refused a second term. He was best known as the Commander in Chief of the Colonial Army, and remembered as the Father of our country. In 1754, Washington began his service with the Virginia Militia as a colonel. He served in the Ohio Valley before being asked to aid the British in the French and Indian War. He led in many battles in both wars but was never seriously wounded when he led charges. Even while musket balls hit his clothing numerous times, as well the horses he rode fell beneath him on occasion; he somehow endured all the battles. George Washington's family had thought him dead in the war at Monongahela, and that he even gave a dying speech. He wrote his brother a letter assuring him that he wasn't dead, and that he had not composed a dying speech till then! He had six white horses in his stable. He and his men won victories in Boston, Trenton, Princeton, and endured defeats as well, but he maintained himself as an effective leader even during the harsh winters and enduring diminishing numbers of troops. Enlisting troops was especially difficult, but he created and offered monetary rewards, lands, and freedom for slaves who fought with him and persevered the duration of the war. During the battle at Yorktown, with the help of French ships, his army won the final and decisive battle, and successfully negotiated surrender with the British.

Noteworthy: The states of Ohio, Indiana, Illinois, Michigan, Wisconsin, and Iowa prohibited slavery because of Congressional act, authored by Constitutional signer Rufus King-and signed into law by President George Washington who was an advocate for prohibiting slavery in those territories. Quote: "I can only say that there is not a man living who wishes more sincerity than I do to see a plan adopted for the abolition of it," (slavery).

In Washington's first Inaugural Address in 1789, he said America's law must be based on the private morality of its citizens; and that morality, in turn, must be based on biblical principles--."

His Faith: Revisionists suppose that since he used many terms for God that he was somehow irreligious or a deist. This evaluation of his true beliefs is not honest or accurate. Washington's terms for God varied from "Divine Author of our blessed Religion," to "the Almighty Being who rules over the Universe." John P. Riley said, Washington viewed the Supreme Being as an overseer and protector of all men, not simply the God of Presbyterians, Episcopalians, or Baptists. Another attack from revisionists who say he did not mention or write of Christian or Jesus Christ. This historical fallacy is easily debunked by reading a single document (a well known handwritten prayer book that was found after his death). The name "Jesus Christ was directly used sixteen times, and numerous other times used in varied forms (e.g., "Jesus, "Lord Jesus," ect), (pg. 270, Original Intent, author David Barton). Revisionists also omit eyewitnesses and testimonies. Washington's daughter said of him "I should have thought it the greatest heresy to doubt his {George Washington's} firm belief in Christianity. His life, his writings prove that he was a Christian." Gunning Bedford, signer of the Constitution said of him, "To the character of hero and patriot, this good man that of Christian…although the man upon the earth, he disdained not to humble himself before his God and to trust in the mercies of Christ." John Marshall, Revolutionary General: Secretary of State; Chief-Justice U.S. Supreme Court, said "He (Washington) was a sincere believer in the Christian faith and a truly devout man."

Interesting Facts on Washington:
- Only founding father to free his slaves.
- Washington rejected a movement among army officers to make him a king.
- He loved fishing and fox hunting.
- He was home schooled by his father and brother.
- He never lived in the White House, the place named after him (Washington D.C.).

Washington left no direct descendant. His stepdaughter Patsy Custis died of epilepsy in 1773. His stepson Jackie Custis died of meningitis. Washington personally witnessed these deaths.

At Washington's death bed he said to his doctor and friend, "Doctor, I die hard, but I am not afraid to go. I believed, from my first attack, that I should not survive it. My breath cannot last long. "His last words were, "Tis well."

John Adams

Short Biography: John Adams was the eldest of three sons, born October 30, 1736 in Quincy, Massachusetts. His family roots come from a generation of Puritans, who came to the new land in the 1630's. John Adams became the second President of the United States, serving March 4, 1797 - March 4, 1801. Before becoming President he served as a lawyer, statesman, diplomat and political theorist. While being a lawyer in Boston he represented Enlightenment values. He was a Federalist and considered a prominent founding father of the United States. He helped immensely in persuading Congress to declare independence from Great Britain. He greatly enhanced the eventual peace treaty with Britain as well.

Major Accomplishments as President:
- built up U.S. Navy
- fought the Quasi War with France 1798-1800
- signed Alien & Sedition Acts 1798
- ended war with France using keen diplomacy
- appointed John Marshall to Supreme Court 1801

His Faith: Adams was considered a Congregationalist. The Congregationalists of that time were leaning Unitarian, and thus he became a Christian Unitarian. The central tenets of the Christian Unitarian Church at that period accepted Jesus Christ as the redeemer of humanity and the Biblical accounts of his miracles as true.

Quotes from Adams:

Suppose a nation in some distant region should take the Bible for their only law book and every member should regulate his conduct by precepts there exhibited...what a Utopia, what a paradise would this region be. I have examined all religions...and the result is that the Bible is the best book in the world. It contains more of my little philosophy that all the libraries I have seen.

The general principles on which the Fathers achieved independence were...the general principles of Christianity...I will avow that I then believed, and now believe, that those general principles of Christianity are as eternal and immutable as the existence and attributes of God, and those principles of liberty are as unalterable as human nature.

The idea of infidelity (a disbelief in the inspiration of the scripture or the divine origin of Christianity) cannot be treated with too much resentment or too much horror. The man who can think of it with patience is a traitor in his heart and ought to be execrated (denounced) as one who adds the deepest hypocrisy to the blackest treason. {A clear denouncement of atheism by Adams}.

Interesting Facts on Adams:

A captain reported to John Adams after a battle for a fort. He told Adams "the fort was handed over to Allen--without the loss of a single life." On June 12th, Congress declared a Day of Prayer and Fasting of which John Adams told his wife Abigail.

History tells us that Adams and Jefferson had a unique relationship, but often tested. Adams was a farmers son, a bit confrontational and humorous, whereas Jefferson was an aristocrat and mostly serious. During the Revolutionary War they were friends and both had an undying devotion to their country. Later as both had aspirations of becoming president, they became archrivals. But, before their lives came to an end they became friends again. Incredibly both died on the same day; July 4th 1826.

Adams journeyed a dangerous voyage on the frigate Boston in 1778, and completed a trek over the Pyrenees.

Adams has lived longer than any President.

Thomas Jefferson

Short Biography: Thomas Jefferson was born on April 13, 1743, and died on July 4, 1826. He was our third President of the United States serving from 1801 thru 1809, and the principal author of the Declaration of Independence in 1776. He was an influential Founding Father, and Jefferson envisioned America as a great Empire of Liberty that would promote republicanism.

Jefferson's Contribution to Promoting Christianity: Jefferson supported provisions and other treaties. Two similar treaties were enacted during Jefferson's administration. One with the Wyandotte Indians and other tribes in 1806, and one with the Cherokees in 1807. In 1787, another act of Congress ordained special lands "for the sole use of Christian Indians" and reserved lands for the Moravian Brethren "for civilizing the Indians and promoting Christianity...." Congress extended this act three times during Jefferson's administration and each time {Jefferson} signed the extension into law.

Jefferson's Contribution to the Constitution: Quote: "On receiving it {the Constitution while in France} I wrote strongly to Mr. Madison urging the want of provision for the freedom of religion, freedom of the press, trial by jury, habeas corpus, the substition of militia for a standing army, and an express reservation to the State of all rights not specifically granted to the Union....This is all the hand I had in what related to the Constitution."

Author Comments on "Separation of Church and State." The separation of church and state as interpreted by contemporary courts currently are not compatible with the Founders' purpose for the First Amendment. "The Founders intended only to prevent the establishment of a single national denomination, not to suppress or restrain public religious expressions," (quote from David Barton). But activist judges have re-interpreted the words of Thomas Jefferson to make unjust laws against religious liberty. Jefferson said, "I consider the government of the United States (the Federal Government) as interdicted by the Constitution from intermeddling with religion institutions, their doctrines, discipline, or exercises." This results not only from the provision that no law shall be made respecting the establishment or free exercise of religion {the First Amendment}, but from that also which reserves to the States the powers not delegated to the United States {The Tenth Amendment}. Certainly, no power to prescribe any religious exercise or to assume authority in any religious discipline has been delegated to the general {Federal} government, (it must then rest with the States). Jefferson made it clear that States could have their own state-established denomination and encouraged religious teaching in general. But it should be noted that the Founders were concerned over the aspect of Catholic doctrine that advocated and led an individual to swear an oath of allegiance to a foreign power (the Pope). But the Founders were not opposed to Catholics as individuals, and they were appreciative of their loyalty for those who fought in the Revolutionary War. The Roman Catholic Church was not prominent during the founding of our country, as most churches were Protestant. There was one Catholic who signed the U.S. Constitution; his name was (Charles Carroll). The Founders wanted a balance of power among religions as understood by a provision stated in New Hampshire Constitution: And every denomination of Christian.... shall be equally under the protection of the law, and no subordination of any one sect or denomination to another be establishment by law. Benjamin Franklin and Thomas Jefferson believed that Christianity was the strongest civil code to curb uncivil behavior. They believed that Christianity best stops the internal motivations for (lust, hate, excessive pride, or anger) which are the seeds of uncivil behavior. Whereas, other religions and civil law only focus on stopping the act.

Thomas Jefferson: Deist or Christian?
By D. James Kennedy

Thomas Jefferson, as we all know, was a skeptic, a man so hostile to Christianity that he scissored from his Bible all references to miracles. He was, as the Freedom from Religion Foundation tells us, "a Deist, opposed to orthodox Christianity and the supernatural."

Or was he? While Jefferson has been lionized by those who seek to drive religion from public life, the true Thomas Jefferson is anything but their friend. He was anything but irreligious, anything but an enemy to Christian faith. Our nation's third president was, in fact, a student of Scripture who attended church regularly and was an active member of the Anglican Church, where he served on his local vestry. He was married in church, sent his children and a nephew to a Christian school, and gave his money to support many different congregations and Christian causes.

Moreover, his "Notes on Religion," nine documents Jefferson wrote in 1776, are "very orthodox statements about the inspiration of Scripture and Jesus as the Christ," according to Mark Beliles, a Providence Foundation scholar and author of an enlightening essay on Jefferson's religious life.

So what about the Jefferson Bible, miracles-free version of the Scriptures? That, too is a myth. It's not a Bible, but an abridgement of the Gospels created by Jefferson in 1804 for the benefit of the Indian's. Jefferson's "Philosophy of Jesus of Nazareth Extracted from the New Testament for the Use of the Indian's" was a tool to evangelize and educate American Indians. There is no evidence that it was an expression of his skepticism.

Jefferson, who gave his money to assist missionary work among the Indians, believed his "abridgement of the New Testament for use of the Indians" would help civilize and educate America's aboriginal inhabitants. Nor did Jefferson cut all miracles from his work, as Beliles points out. While the original manuscript no longer exists, the Table of Texts that survives includes several accounts of Christ's healings.

But didn't Jefferson believe in the complete separation of church and state? After all, Jefferson's 1802 letter to the Baptists in Danbury, Conn in which he cited the First Amendment's creation of a "wall of separation" between church and state is an ACLU proof-text for its claim that the First Amendment makes the public square a religion-free zone. But if the ACLU is right, why, just two days after he sent his letter to the Danbury Baptist did President Jefferson attend public worship services in the US Capitol buildings, something he did throughout his two terms in office? And why did he authorize the use of the War Office and the Treasury building for church services in Washington D.C.?

Jefferson's outlook on religion and government is more fully revealed in another 1802 letter in which he wrote that he did not want his administration to be a "government without religion" but one that would "strengthen religious freedom."

Jefferson was a true friend of the Christian faith. But was he a true Christian? A nominal Christian—as demonstrated by his lifelong practice of attending worship services, reading the Bible and following the moral principles of Christ—Jefferson was not, in my opinion, a genuine Christian. In 1813, after his public career was over, Jefferson rejected the deity of Christ. Like so many millions of church me members today, he was outwardly religious, but never experienced the new birth that Jesus told Nicodemus was necessary to enter the kingdom of Heaven.

Nonetheless, Jefferson's presidential acts would, if done today, send the ACLU marching into court. He signed legislation that gave land to Indian missionaries, put chaplains on the government payroll, and provided for the punishment of irreverent solders. He also sent Congress an Indian treaty that set aside money for a priest's salary and for the construction of a church.

Most intriguing is the manner of which Jefferson dated an official document. Instead of "in the year of our Lord," Jefferson used the phrase "in the year of our Lord Christ." Christian historian David Barton has the proof—the original document signed by Jefferson of the 'eighteenth day of October in the year of our Lord Christ, 1804."

The Supreme Court ruled in 1947 that Jefferson's wall of separation between church and state "must be kept high and impregnable. We could not approve the slightest breach." Judging from the record, it looks like the wall some say Tom built is, in fact, the wall Tom breached.

The real Thomas Jefferson, it turns out, is the ACLU's worst nightmare.

James Madison

Bio: President was born on March 16, 1751, and died on June 28, 1836. He was the fourth President of the United States serving during the years of 1809 - 1817. He is considered the "Father of the Constitution," and the key author of the U.S. Bill of Rights. His influence along with Alexander Hamilton and John Jay produced the Federalist Papers in 1788 which was most influential for the defense of the Constitution.

He was considered a political theorist because he believed in the separation of powers federal state governments (federalism) and written the federal government (Checks and balances) to protect individual rights. In 1789, Madison became a leader in the new House of Representatives. Notably he dropped the first ten Amendments to the Constitution. Madison also supervised the Louisiana Purchase, doubling the nation's size. Madison was President when he led the into the War of 1812. The war was declared due to the British. Madison eventually helped in the developing of the nation by his administrative organization by promoting a stronger government and military, and a national bank.

Interesting Facts:
- At age 16 studied under Reverend Thomas Martin.
- He attended the college of New Jersey (Now Princeton University)
- He studied Latin - Greek - science - geography - mathematics - rhetoric & philosophy/Continued at Princeton studying Hebrew and political philosophy.
- Madison and other Founding Fathers organized three branches of government (a key element in Constitution)

Famous Quote: "You must first enable the government to control the government and in the next place, oblique it to control itself."

Cont. Quote: "I do therefore issue this my proclamation, recommending to all who be piously disposed to write their hearts and vows in addressing at one and the same their vows and adorations to the Giant Parent and Sovereign of the Universe...to render Him thanks for all the many blessings He has bestowed on the people of the United States."

Important Decisions: Early in his career Madison made (6) important decisions promoting the Christian Faith:

1. Madison desired that act public official to declare openly and publicly their Christian beliefs and testimony.

2. Madison was a member of the Committee with authoring the 1776 Virginia Bill of Rights declaring that "It is the duty of all to practice Christian fore bearance, love and charity toward each other.

3. Madison proposed wording for the first Amendment demonstrates that he opposed only the establishment of a federal denominating not public religious activities. His proposal: The civil rights of none shall be abridged on account of religious belief or worship, nor shall any national religion be established.

4. In 1812 authorized and approval selected congressional chaplains.

5. In 1812 Madison signed a federal bill aiding a Bible society's mass distribution of the Bible.

6. Throughout his presidency (1809- 1816) Madison publicly endorsed proclamation of National days of prayer, fasting, and thanksgiving.

CHAPTER 10

A GLANCE AT OUR FOREFATHERS

Founding Fathers as Christians {quotes}

Samuel Adams: Father of the American Revolution, Signer of the Declaration of independence
recommend my Soul to that Almighty Being who gave it, and my body I commit to the dust, relying upon the merits of Jesus Christ for a pardon of all my sins.

Charles Carroll: Signer of the Declaration of Independence
On the mercy of my Redeemer I rely for salvation and on His merits; not on the works I have done in obedience to His precepts.

First Associate Justice Appointed by George Washington to the Supreme Court
Sensible of my mortality, but being of sound mind, after recommending my soul to Almighty God through the merits of my Redeemer and my body to the earth...

John Dickinson: Signer of the Constitution

Rendering thanks to my Creator for my existence and station among His works, for my birth in a country enlightened by the Gospel and enjoying freedom, and for all His other kindnesses, to Him I resign myself, humbly confiding in His goodness and in His mercy through Jesus Christ for the events of eternity.

John Hancock: Signer of the Declaration of Independence

I John Hancock,... being advanced in years and being of perfect mind and memory-thanks be given to God therefore calling to mind the mortality of my body and knowing it is appointed for all men once to [Hebrews 9:27], do make and ordain this my last will and testament... Principally and first of all, I give and recommend my soul into the hands of God that gave it: and my body I recommend to the earth... nothing doubting but at the general resurrection I shall receive the same again by the mercy and power of God...

Patrick Henry: Governor of Virginia, and Patriot

This is all the inheritance I can give to my dear family. The religion of Christ can give them one which will make them rich indeed.

John Jay: First Chief Justice of the US Supreme Court

Unto Him who is the author and giver of all good, I render sincere and humble thanks for His manifold and unmerited blessings, and especially for our redemption and salvation by His beloved son. He has been pleased to bless me with excellent parents, with a virtuous wife, and with worthy children. His protection has companied me through many eventful years, faithfully employed in the service of my country; His providence has not only conducted me to this tranquil situation but also given me abundant reason to be contented and thankful. Blessed be His holy name!

Daniel St. Thomas Jenifer: Signer of the Constitution
In the name of God, Amen. I, Daniel of Saint Thomas Jenifer... of disposing mind and memory, commend my soul to my blessed Redeemer...

Henry Knox: Revolutionary War General, Secretary of War
First, I think it proper to express my unshaken opinion of the immortality of my soul or mind; and to dedicate and devote the same to the supreme head of the Universe- to that great and tremendous Jehovah, -Who created the universal frame of nature, worlds, and systems in number infinite... To this awfully sublime Being do I resign my spirit with unlimited confidence of His mercy and protection...

John Langdon: Signer of the Constitution
In the name of God, Amen. I, John Langdon,... considering the uncertainty of life and that it is appointed unto all men once to die [Hebrews 9:27], do make, ordain and publish this my last will and testament in marmer following, that is to say-First: I commend my soul to the infmite mercies of God in Christ Jesus, the beloved Son of the Father, who died and rose again that He might be the Lord of the dead and of the living... professing to believe and hope in the joyful Scripture doctrine of a resurrection to eternal life...

John Morton: Signer of the Declaration of Independence
With an awful reverence to the great Almighty God, Creator of all mankind, I, John Morton... being sick and weak in body but of sound mind and memory- thanks be given to Almighty God for the same, for all

His mercies and favors-and considering the certainty of death and the uncertainty of the times thereof, do, for the settling of such temporal estate as it hath pleased God to bless me with in this life...

Robert Treat Paine: Signer of the Declaration of Independence

I desire to bless and praise the name of God most high for appointing me my birth in a land of Gospel Light where the glorious tidings of a Savior and of pardon and salvation through Him have been continually sounding in mine ears. From "The Papers of Robert Treat Paine," Stephen Riley and Edward Hanson, editors. (Boston: Massachusetts Historical Society, 1992), Vol. I, p. 48, March/April, 1749. When I consider that this instrument contemplates my departure from this life and all earthly enjoyments and my entrance on another state of existence, I am constrained to express my adoration of the Supreme Being, the Author of my existence, in full belief of his providential goodness and his forgiving mercy revealed to the world through Jesus Christ, through whom I hope for never ending happiness in a future state, acknowledging with grateful remembrance the happiness I have enjoyed in my passage through a long life...

Charles Cotesworth Pinckney: Signer of the Constitution

To the eternal, immutable, and only true God be all honor and glory, now and forever, Amen!

Rufus Putnam: Revolutionary War General, First Surveyor General of the United States

First, I give my soul to a holy, sovereign God Who gave it in humble hope of a blessed immortality through the atonement and righteousness of Jesus Christ and the sanctifying grace of the Holy Spirit. My body I commit to the earth to be buried in a decent Christian manner. I fully believe that this body shall, by the mighty power of God, be raised to life at the last day; 'for this corruptible must put on incorruption and this mortal must put on immortality.' [I Corinthians 15:53]

Benjamin Rush: Signer of the Declaration of Independence

My only hope of salvation is in the infinite, transcendent love of God manifested to the world by the death of His Son upon the cross. Nothing but His blood will wash away my sins. I rely exclusively upon it. Come, Lord Jesus! Come quickly!

Roger Sherman: Signer of the Declaration of Independence, Signer of the Constitution

I believe that there is one only living and true God, existing in three persons, the Father, the Son, and the Holy Ghost.... that the Scriptures of the Old and New Testaments are a revelation from God.... that God did send His own Son to become man, die in the room and stead of sinners, and thus to lay a foundation for the offer of pardon and salvation to all mankind so as all may be saved who are willing to accept the Gospel offer.

Richard Stockton: Signer of the Declaration of Independence

I think it proper here not only to subscribe to the entire belief of the great and leading doctrines of the Christian religion, such as the Being of God, the universal defection and depravity of human nature, the divinity of the person and completeness of the redemption purchased by the blessed Savior, the necessity of the operations of the Divine Spirit, of Divine Faith, accompanied with an habitual virtuous life, and the universality of the dine Providence, but also... that the fear of God is the beginning of wisdom; that the way of life held up in the Christian system is calculated for the most complete happiness that can be enjoyed in this mortal state; that all occasions of vice and immorality is injurious either immediately or consequentially, even in this life; that as Almighty God hath not been pleased in the Holy Scriptures to prescribe any precise mode in which He is to be publicly worshiped, all contention about it generally arises from want of knowledge or want of virtue.

Jonathan Trumbull Sr.: Governor of Connecticut, Patriot

Principally and first of all, I bequeath my soul to God the Creator and Giver thereof, and body to the Earth... nothing doubting but that I shall receive the same again at the General Resurrection through the power of Almighty God; believing and hoping for eternal life through the merits of my dear, exalted Redeemer Jesus Christ, if you are not clothed with the spotless robe of His righteousness, you must forever perish.

{Note: this list of Founding Fathers quotes is from personal wills, autographed letters and documents, and is not an exhaustive list.}

THE DECLARATION OF INDEPENDENCE
07/04/1776

When in the course of human events, it becomes necessary for one people to dissolve the political bands which have connected them with another, and to assume among the powers of the earth the separate and equal station to which the laws of nature and of nature's God entitles them, a decent respect to the opinions of mankind requires that they should declare the causes which impel them to the separation.

We hold these truths to be self-evident, that all men are created equal, that they are endowed by their Creator with certain unalienable rights that among these are life, liberty and the pursuit of happiness. That to secure these rights, governments are instituted among men, deriving their just powers from the consent of the governed. That whenever any form of government becomes destructive of these ends, it is the right of the people to alter or to abolish it and to institute new government, laying its foundation on such principles and organizing its powers in such form as to them shall seem most likely to affect their safety and happiness. Prudence, indeed, will dictate that governments long established should not be changed for light and transient causes; and accordingly, all experience hath shown that mankind are more disposed to suffer while evils are sufferable than to right themselves by abolishing the forms to which they are accustomed. But when a long train of abuses and usurpations, pursuing invariably the same object, evinces a design to reduce them under absolute despotism, it is their right, it is their duty, to throw off such government and to provide new guards for their future security. Such has been the patient sufferance of these Colonies; and such is now the necessity which constrains them to alter their former systems of governments. The history of the present King of Great Britain is a history of repeated injuries and usurpations, all having in direct object the establishment of an absolute tyranny over these States. To prove this, let facts be submitted to a candid world.

He has refused his assent to laws, the most wholesome and necessary for the public good.

He has forbidden his Governors to pass laws of immediate and pressing importance, unless suspended in their operation till his assent should be obtained; and when so suspended, he has utterly neglected to attend to them.

He has refused to pass other laws for the accommodation of large districts of people unless those people would relinquish the right of representation in the legislature, a right inestimable to them and formidable to tyrants only.

He has called together legislative bodies at places unusual, uncomfortable, and distant from the depository of their public records, for the sole purpose of fatiguing them into compliance with his measures.

He has dissolved representative Houses repeatedly for opposing with manly firmness his invasion on the rights of the people.

He has refused for a long time, after such dissolutions, to cause others to be elected; whereby the legislative powers, incapable of annihilation, have returned to the people at large for their exercise; the State remaining in the meantime exposed to all the dangers of invasion from without and convulsions within.

He has endeavored to prevent the population of these States; for that purpose obstructing the laws for naturalization of foreigners; refusing to pass others to encourage their migrations hither, and raising the conditions of new appropriations of lands.

He has obstructed the administration of justice by refusing his assent to laws for establishing judiciary powers.

He has made judges dependent on his will alone for the tenure of their offices and the amount and payment of their salaries.

He has erected a multitude of new offices and sent hither swarms of officers to harass our people and eat out their substance.

He has kept among us, in times of peace, standing armies without the consent of our legislature.

He has affected to render the military independent of and superior to the civil power.

He has combined with others to subject us to a jurisdiction foreign to our Constitution and unacknowledged by our laws; giving his assent to their acts of pretended legislation:

For quartering large bodies of armed troops among us:

For protecting them, by a mock trial, from punishment for any murders which they should commit on the inhabitants of these States:

For cutting off our trade with all parts of the world:

For imposing taxes on us without our consent:

For depriving us in many cases of the benefits of trial by jury:

For transporting us beyond seas to be tried for pretended offenses:

For abolishing the free system of English laws in a neighboring province, establishing therein an arbitrary government, and enlarging its boundaries so as to ren-der it at once an example and fit instrument for introducing the same absolute rule into these Colonies:

For taking away our charters, abolishing our most valuable laws, and altering fundamentally the forms of our governments:

For suspending our own legislatures, and declaring themselves invested with power to legislate for us in all cases whatsoever.

He has abdicated government here, by declaring us out of his protection and waging war against us.

He has plundered our seas, ravaged our coasts, burnt our towns, and destroyed the lives of our people.

He is at this time transporting large armies of foreign mercenaries to complete the works of death, desolation and tyranny, already begun with circumstances of cruelty and perfidy scarcely paralleled in the most barbarous ages, and totally unworthy the head of a civilized nation.

He has constrained our fellow citizens taken captive on the high Seas to bear Arms against their country, to become the executioners of their friends and brethren, or to fall themselves by their hands.

He has excited domestic insurrections amongst us, and has endeavoured to bring on the inhabitants of our frontiers, the merciless Indian savages, whose known rule of warfare, is an undistinguished destruction of all ages, sexes and conditions.

In every stage of these oppressions we have petitioned for redress in the most humble terms: Our repeated petitions have been answered only by repeated injury. A Prince whose character is thus marked by every act which may define a tyrant, is unfit to be the ruler of a free people.

Nor have we been wanting in attentions to our British brethren. We have warned them from time to time of attempts by their legislature to extend an unwarrantable jurisdiction over us. We have reminded them of the circumstances of our emigration and settlement here. We have appealed to their native justice and magnanimity and we have conjured them by the ties of our common kindred to disavow these usurpations which would inevitably interrupt our connections and correspondence. They, too, have been deaf to the voice of justice and of consanguinity. We must, therefore, acquiesce in the necessity which denounces our separation and hold them, as we hold the rest of mankind, enemies in war, in peace friends.

We, therefore, the Representatives of the United States of America, in general Congress assembled, appealing to the Supreme Judge of the world for the rectitude of our intentions, do, in the name and by the authority of the good people of these Colonies, solemnly publish and declare that these United Colonies are, and of right ought to be, free and independent States; that they are absolved from all allegiance to the British Crown and that all political connection between them and the State of Great Britain is and ought to be totally dissolved; and that as free and independent States, they have full power to levy war, conclude peace, contract alliance, establish commerce, and do all other acts and things which independent States may of right do. And for the support of this Declaration, with a firm reliance on the protection of Divine Providence, we mutually pledge to each other our lives, our fortunes, and our sacred honor.

Signers of the Declaration of Independence

NEW HAMPSHIRE: Josiah Bartlett, William Whipple, Matthew Thornton

MASSACHUSETTS: John Hancock, John Adams, Samuel Adams, Robert Treat Paine

RHODE ISLAND: Elbridge Gerry, Stephen Hopkins, William Ellery

CONNECTICUT: Roger Sherman, Samuel Huntington, William Williams, Oliver Wolcott

NEW YORK: William Floyd, Philip Livingston, Francis Lewis, Lewis Morris

NEW JERSEY: Richard Stockton, John Witherspoon, Francis Hopkinson, John Hart, Abraham Clark

PENNSYLVANIA: Robert Morris, Benjamin Rush, Benjamin Franklin, John Morton, George Clymer, James Smith, George Taylor, James Wilson, George Ross

DELAWARE: Ceasar Rodney, George Read, Thomas McKean

MARYLAND: Samuel Chase, Thomas Stone, William Paca, Charles Carroll of Carrollton

VIRGINIA: George Wythe, Richard Henry Lee, Thomas Jefferson,

Benjamin Harrison, Thomas Nelson, Jr., Francis Lightfoot Lee, Carter Braxton

NORTH CAROLINA: William Hooper, Joseph Hewes, John Penn

SOUTH CAROLINA: Edward Rutledge, Thomas Heyward, Jr., Thomas Lynch, Jr., Authur Middleton

GEORGIA: Button Gwinnett, Lyman Hall, George Walton
  *http://wallbuilders.com/LIBissuesArticles.asp?id=25685

CONSTITUTION OF THE UNITED STATES OF AMERICA

Preamble

We the people of the United States, in order to form a more perfect Union, establish justice, insure domestic tranquility, provide for the common defense, promote the general welfare, and secure the blessings of liberty to ourselves and our posterity, do ordain and establish this Constitution for the United States of America.

Article 1

Section 1. All legislative powers herein granted shall be vested in a Congress of the United States which shall consist of a Senate and House of Representatives.

Section 2. The House of Representatives shall be composed of members chosen every second year by the people of the several States, and the electors in each State shall have the qualifications requisite for electors of the most numerous branch of the State legislature.

No person shall be a Representative who shall not have attained to the age of twenty-five years and been seven years a citizen of the United States, and who shall not, when elected, be an inhabitant of that State in which he shall be chosen.

Representatives and direct taxes shall be apportioned among the several States which may be included within this Union, according to their respective numbers, which shall be determined by adding to the whole number of free persons, including those bound to service for a term of years, and excluding Indians not taxed, three fifths of all other persons. [The preceding portion in italics is amended by the Fourteenth Amendment, Section 2.] The actual enumeration shall be made within three years after the first meeting of the Congress of the United States, and within every subsequent term of ten years, in such manner as they shall by law direct. The number of Representatives shall not exceed one for every thirty thousand but each State shall have at least one Representative; and until such enumeration shall be made, the State of New Hampshire shall be entitled to choose three, Massachusetts eight, Rhode Island and Providence Plantations one, Connecticut five, New York six; New Jersey four, Pennsylvania eight, Delaware one, Maryland six, Virginia ten, North Carolina five, South Carolina five, and Georgia three.

When vacancies happen in the representation from any State, the executive authority thereof shall issue writs of election to fill such vacancies.

The House of Representatives shall choose their Speaker and other officers; and shall have the sole power of impeachment.

Section 3. The Senate of the United States shall be composed of two Senators from each State, chosen by the legislature thereof, for six years; and each Senator shall have one vote.

Immediately after they shall be assembled in consequence of the first election, they shall be divided as equally as may be into three classes. The seats of the Senators of the first class shall be vacated at the expiration of the second year, of the second class at the expiration of the fourth year, and of the third class at the expiration of the sixth year, so that one-third may be chosen every second year; and if vacancies happen by resignation, or otherwise, during the recess of the legislature of any State, the Executive thereof may make temporary appointments until the next meeting of the legislature, which shall then fill such vacancies.

No person shall be a Senator who shall not have attained to the age of thirty years and been nine years a citizen of the United States, and who shall not, when elected, be an inhabitant of that State for which he shall be chosen.

The Vice-President of the United States shall be President of the Senate but shall have no vote unless they be equally divided.

The Senate shall choose their other officers, and also a President pro tempore, in the absence of the Vice-President, or when he shall exercise the office of President of the United States.

The Senate shall have the sole power to try all impeachments. When sitting for that purpose, they shall be on oath or affirmation. When the President of the United States is tried, the Chief Justice shall preside: and no person shall be convicted without the concurrence of two thirds of the members present.

Judgment in cases of impeachment shall not extend further than to removal from office and disqualification to hold and enjoy any office of honor, trust, or profit under the United States: but the party convicted shall nevertheless be liable and subject to indictment, trial, judgment and punishment according to Law.

Section 4. The times, places, and manner of holding elections for Senators and Representatives shall be prescribed in each State by the legislature thereof; but the Congress may at any time by law make or alter such regulations except as to the places of choosing Senators.

The Congress shall assemble at least once in every year, and such meeting shall be on the first Monday in December, unless they shall by law appoint a different day.

Section 5. Each House shall be the judge of the elections, returns, and qualifications of its own members, and a majority of each shall constitute a quorum to do business; but a smaller number may adjourn from day to day and may be authorized to compel the attendance of absent members, in such manner, and under such penalties as each House may provide.

Each House may determine the rules of its proceedings, punish its members for disorderly behavior, and, with the concurrence of two thirds, expel a member.

Each House shall keep a journal of its proceedings and from time to time publish the same, excepting such parts as may in their judgment require secrecy; and the yeas and nays of the members of either House on any question shall, at the desire of one fifth of those present, be entered on the Journal.

Neither House, during the session of Congress, shall, without the consent of the other, adjourn for more than three days nor to any other place than that in which the two Houses shall be sitting.

Section 6. The Senators and Representatives shall receive a compensation for their services, to be ascertained by law, and paid out of the Treasury of the United States. They shall in all cases except treason, felony, and breach of the peace, be privileged from arrest during their attendance at the session of their respective Houses and in going to and returning from the same; and for any speech or debate in either House they shall not be questioned in any other place.

No Senator or Representative shall, during the time for which he was elected, be appointed to any civil office under the authority of the United States which shall have been created or the emoluments whereof shall have been increased during such time; and no person holding any office under the United States shall be a member of either House during his continuance in office.

Section 7. All bills for raising revenue shall originate in the House of Representatives; but the Senate may propose or concur with amendments as on other bills.

Every bill which shall have passed the House of Representatives and the Senate shall, before it becomes a law, be presented to the President of the United States; if he approve, he shall sign it, but if not he shall return it, with his objections, to that House in which it shall have originated, who shall enter the objections at large on their journal and proceed to reconsider it. If, after such reconsideration, two thirds of that House shall agree to pass the bill, it shall be sent, together with the objections, to the other House, by which it shall likewise be reconsidered, and if approved by two thirds of that House, it shall become a law. But in all such cases, the votes of both Houses shall be determined by yeas and nays and the names of the persons voting for and against the bill shall be entered on the journal of each House respectively. If any bill shall not be returned by the President within ten days (Sundays excepted) after it shall have been presented to him, the same shall be a law in like manner as if he had signed it unless the Congress, by their adjournment, prevent its return, in which case it shall not be a law.

Every order, resolution, or vote to which the concurrence of the Senate and House of Representatives may be necessary (except on a question of adjournment) shall be presented to the President of the United States; and before the same shall take effect shall be approved by him, or, being disapproved by him, shall be repassed by two thirds of the Senate and House of Representatives according to the rules and limitations prescribed in the case of a bill.

Section 8. The Congress shall have power to lay and collect taxes, duties, imposts, and excises to pay the debts and provide for the common defense and general welfare of the United States; but all duties, imposts, and excises shall be uniform throughout the United States;

To borrow money on the credit of the United States;

To regulate commerce with foreign nations and among the several States and with the Indian tribes;

To establish an uniform rule of naturalization and uniform laws on the subject of bankruptcies throughout the United States;

To coin money, regulate the value thereof and of foreign coin, and fix the standard of weights and measures;

To provide for the punishment of counterfeiting the securities and current coin of the United States;

To establish post offices and post roads;

To promote the progress of science and useful arts by securing for limited times to authors and inventors the exclusive rights to their respective writings and discoveries;

To constitute tribunals inferior to the Supreme Court;

To define and punish piracies and felonies committed on the high seas and offences against the law of nations;

To declare war, grant letters of marque and reprisal, and make rules concerning captures on land and water;

To raise & support armies, but no appropriation of money to that use shall be for a longer term than two years;

To provide and maintain a Navy;

To make rules for the government and regulation of the land and naval forces;

To provide for calling forth the militia to execute the laws of the Union, suppress insurrections, and repel invasions;

To provide for organizing, arming, and disciplining the militia and for governing such part of them as may be employed in the service of the United States, reserving to the States respectively the appointment of the officers and the authority of training the militia according to the discipline prescribed by Congress;

To exercise exclusive legislation in all cases whatsoever over such district (not exceeding ten miles square) as may, by cession of particular States and the acceptance of Congress, become the seat of the government of the United States, and to exercise like authority over all places purchased by the consent of the legislature of the State in which the same shall be for the erection of forts, magazines, arsenals, dockyards, and other needful buildings; – and

To make all laws which shall be necessary and proper for carrying into execution the foregoing powers and all other powers vested by this Constitution in the government of the United States or in any department or officer thereof.

Section 9. The migration or importation of such persons as any of the States now existing shall think proper to admit shall not be prohibited by the Congress prior to the year one thousand eight hundred and eight, but a tax or duty may be imposed on such importation not exceeding ten dollars for each person.

The privilege of the writ of Habeas Corpus shall not be suspended unless when in cases of rebellion or invasion the public safety may require it.

No bill of attainder or ex post facto law shall be passed.

No capitation or other direct tax shall be laid unless in proportion to the census or enumeration herein before directed to be taken.

No tax or duty shall be laid on articles exported from any State.

No preference shall be given by any regulation of commerce or revenue to the ports of one State over those of another: nor shall vessels bound to or from one State be obliged to enter, clear, or pay duties in another.

No money shall be drawn from the Treasury but in consequence of appropriations made by law; and a regular statement and account of the receipts and expenditures of all public money shall be published from time to time.

No title of nobility shall be granted by the United States: and no person holding any office of profit or trust under them shall, without the consent of the Congress, accept of any present, emolument, office, or title of any kind whatever from any king, prince, or foreign State.

Section 10. No State shall enter into any treaty, alliance, or confederation; grant letters of marque and reprisal; coin money, emit bills of credit; make any thing but gold and silver coin a tender in payment of debts; pass any bill of attainder, ex post facto law, or law impairing the obligation of contracts, or grant any title of nobility.

No State shall, without the consent of the Congress, lay any imposts of duties on imports or exports except what may be absolutely necessary for executing its inspection laws: and the net produce of all duties and imposts laid by any State on imports or exports shall be for the use of the Treasury of the United States; and all such laws shall be subject to the revision and control of the Congress.

No State shall, without the consent of Congress, lay any duty of tonnage, keep troops, or ships of war in time of peace, enter into any agreement or compact with another State or with a foreign power, or engage in war, unless actually invaded, or in such imminent danger as will not admit of delay.

Article 2

Section 1. The executive power shall be vested in a President of the United States of America. He shall hold his office during the term of four years and, together with the Vice-President chosen for the same term, be elected as follows:

Each State shall appoint, in such manner as the legislature thereof may direct, a number of electors equal to the whole number of Senators and Representatives to which the State may be entitled in the Congress: but no Senator or Representative or person holding an office of trust or profit under the United States shall be appointed an elector.

The electors shall meet in their respective States and vote by ballot for two persons of whom one at least shall not be an inhabitant of the same State with themselves. And they shall make a list of all the persons voted for and of the number of votes for each; which list they shall sign and certify and transmit sealed to the seat of the government of the United States, directed to the President of the Senate. The President of the Senate shall, in the presence of the Senate and House of Representatives, open all the certificates and the votes shall then be counted. The person having the greatest number of votes shall be the President if such number be a majority of the whole number of electors appointed; and if there be more than one who have such majority and have an equal number of votes, then the House of Representatives shall immediately choose by ballot one of them for President; and if no person have a majority, then from the five highest on the list the said House shall in like manner choose the President. But in choosing the President, the votes shall be taken by States, the representation from each State having one vote; a quorum for this purpose shall consist of a member or members from two-thirds of the States, and a majority of all the States shall be necessary to a choice. In every case, after the choice of the President, the person having the greatest number of votes of the electors shall be the Vice-President. But if there should remain two or more who have equal votes, the Senate shall choose from them by ballot the Vice-President. [The preceding section has been superseded by the Twelfth Amendment.]

The Congress may determine the time of choosing the electors and the day on which they shall give their votes; which day shall be the same throughout the United States.

No person except a natural born citizen, or a citizen of the United States at the time of the adoption of this Constitution, shall be eligible to the office of President; neither shall any person be eligible to that office who shall not have attained to the age of thirty-five years and been fourteen years a resident within the United States.

In case of the removal of the President from office, or of his death, resignation, or inability to discharge the powers and duties of the said office, the same shall devolve on the Vice-President, and the Congress may by law provide for the case of removal, death, resignation, or inability, both of the President and Vice-President, declaring what officer shall then act as President, and such officer shall act accordingly until the disability be removed or a President shall be elected.

The President shall, at stated times, receive for his services a compensation which shall neither be increased nor diminished during the period for which he shall have been elected, and he shall not receive within that period any other emolument from the United States or any of them.

Before he enter on the execution of his office, he shall take the following oath or affirmation: – "I do solemnly swear (or affirm) that I will faithfully execute the office of President of the United States and will, to the best of my ability, preserve, protect, and defend the Constitution of the United States."

Section 2. The President shall be Commander in Chief of the Army and Navy of the United States, and of the militia of the several States when called into the actual service of the United States; he may require the opinion, in writing, of the principal officer in each of the executive departments upon any subject relating to the duties of their respective offices, and he shall have power to grant reprieves and pardons for offenses against the United States, except in cases of impeachment.

He shall have power, by and with the advice and consent of the Senate, to make treaties, provided two thirds of the Senators present concur; and he shall nominate, and by and with the advice and consent of the Senate, shall appoint Ambassadors, other public Ministers and Consuls, Judges of the Supreme Court, and all other Officers of the United States, whose appointments are not herein otherwise provided for and which shall be established by law: but the Congress may by law vest the appointment of such inferior officers as they think proper in the President alone, in the Courts of law, or in the heads of departments.

The President shall have power to fill up all vacancies that may happen during the recess of the Senate by granting commissions which shall expire at the end of their next session.

Section 3. He shall from time to time give to the Congress information of the state of the Union and recommend to their consideration such measures as he shall judge necessary and expedient; he may, on extraordinary occasions, convene both Houses, or either of them, and in case of disagreement between them with respect to the time of adjournment, he may adjourn them to such time as he shall think proper; he shall receive Ambassadors and other public Ministers; he shall take care that the laws be faithfully executed, and shall commission all the officers of the United States.

Section 4. The President, Vice-President, and all civil officers of the United States shall be removed from office on impeachment for and conviction of treason, bribery, or other high crimes and misdemeanors.

Article 3

Section 1. The judicial power of the United States shall be vested in one Supreme Court and in such inferior Courts as the Congress may from time to time ordain and establish. The Judges, both of the Supreme and inferior Courts, shall hold their offices during good behavior and shall, at stated times, receive for their services a compensation which shall not be diminished during their continuance in office.

Section 2. The judicial power shall extend to all cases in law and equity arising under this Constitution, the laws of the United States, and treaties made, or which shall be made, under their authority: – to all cases affecting Ambassadors, other public Ministers and Consuls; – to all cases of admiralty and maritime jurisdiction; – to controversies to which the United States shall be a party; – to controversies between two or more States; – between a State and citizens of another State; – between citizens of different States, – between citizens of the same State claiming lands under grants of different States, and between a State, or the citizens thereof, and foreign States, citizens, or subjects.

In all cases affecting Ambassadors, other public Ministers and Consuls, and those in which a State shall be party, the Supreme Court shall have original jurisdiction. In all the other cases before mentioned, the Supreme Court shall have appellate jurisdiction both as to law and fact with such exceptions and under such regulations as the Congress shall make.

The trial of all crimes, except in cases of impeachment, shall be by jury; and such trial shall be held in the State where the said crimes shall have been committed; but when not committed within any State, the trial shall be at such place or places as the Congress may by law have directed.

Section 3. Treason against the United States shall consist only in levying war against them or in adhering to their enemies, giving them aid and comfort. No person shall be convicted of treason unless on the testimony of two witnesses to the same overt act or on confession in open court.

The Congress shall have power to declare the punishment of treason, but no attainder of treason shall work corruption of blood or forfeiture except during the life of the person attainted.

Article 4

Section 1. Full faith and credit shall be given in each State to the public acts, records, and judicial proceedings of every other State. And the Congress may by general laws prescribe the manner in which such acts, records, and proceedings shall be proved, and the effect thereof.

Section 2. The citizens of each State shall be entitled to all privileges and immunities of citizens in the several States.

A person charged in any State with treason, felony, or other crime, who shall flee from justice and be found in another State, shall on demand of the executive authority of the State from which he fled, be delivered up to be removed to the State having jurisdiction of the crime.

No person held to service or labor in one State under the laws thereof, escaping into another, shall, in consequence of any law or regulation therein, be discharged from such service or labor, but shall be delivered up on claim of the party to whom such service or labor may be due.

Section 3. New States may be admitted by the Congress into this Union; but no new State shall be formed or erected within the jurisdiction of any other State; nor any State be formed by the junction of two or more States or parts of States without the consent of the legislatures of the States concerned as well as of the Congress.

The Congress shall have power to dispose of and make all needful rules and regulations respecting the territory or other property belonging to the United States; and nothing in this Constitution shall be so construed as to prejudice any claims of the United States or of any particular State.

Section 4. The United States shall guarantee to every State in this Union a republican form of government and shall protect each of them against invasion; and on application of the legislature, or of the Executive (when the legislature cannot be convened), against domestic violence.

Article 5

The Congress, whenever two thirds of both Houses shall deem it necessary, shall propose amendments to this Constitution or, on the application of the legislatures of two thirds of the several States, shall call a convention for proposing amendments which, in either case, shall be valid to all intents and purposes as part of this Constitution when ratified by the legislatures of three fourths of the several States or by conventions in three fourths thereof as the one or the other mode of ratification may be proposed by the Congress; provided that no amendment which may be made prior to the year one thousand eight hundred and eight shall in any manner affect the first and fourth clauses in the ninth section of the first article; and that no State, without its consent, shall be deprived of its equal suffrage in the Senate.

Article 6

All debts contracted and engagements entered into before the adoption of this Constitution shall be as valid against the United States under this Constitution as under the Confederation.

This Constitution and the laws of the United States which shall be made in pursuance thereof; and all treaties made or which shall be made, under the authority of the United States shall be the supreme law of the land; and the judges in every State shall be bound thereby, any thing in the Constitution or laws of any State to the contrary notwithstanding.

The Senators and Representatives before mentioned, and the members of the several State legislatures, and all executive and judicial officers both of the United States and of the several States, shall be bound by oath or affirmation to support this Constitution; but no religious test shall ever be required as a qualification to any office or public trust under the United States.

Article 7

The ratification of the conventions of nine States shall be sufficient for the establishment of this Constitution between the States so ratifying the same.

DONE in convention by the unanimous consent of the States present the seventeenth day of September in the Year of our Lord one thousand seven hundred and eighty seven, and of the independence of the United States of America the twelfth.

Signers of the Constitution

DELAWARE : George Read, Gunning Bedford, Jr., John Dickinson, Richard Bassett, Jacob Broom

MARYLAND : James McHenry, Daniel of St. Thomas Jenifer, Daniel Carroll

VIRGINIA : John Blair, James Madison, Jr., George Washington

NORTH CAROLINA : William Blount, Richard Dobbs Spaight, Hugh Williamson

SOUTH CAROLINA : John Rutledge, Charles Cotesworth Pinckney, Charles Pinckney, Pierce Butler

GEORGIA : William Few, Abraham Baldwin

NEW HAMPSHIRE : John Langdon, Nicholas Gilman

MASSACHUSETTS : Nathaniel Gorham, Rufus King

CONNECTICUT : William Samuel Johnson, Roger Sherman

NEW YORK : Alexander Hamilton

NEW JERSEY : William Livingston, David Brearley, William Paterson, Jonathan Dayton

PENNSYLVANIA : Benjamin Franklin, Thomas Mifflin, Robert Morris, George Clymer, Thomas Fitzsimons, Jared Ingersoll, James Wilson, Gouverneur Morris
  *http://wallbuilders.com/LIBissuesArticles.asp?id=36438

www.ingramcontent.com/pod-product-compliance
Lightning Source LLC
Chambersburg PA
CBHW021630120626
46545CB00002B/483